SMART DOLPHIN ZONE

3 three

English for Elementary

by Patricia Avila

DATOS EDITORIALES

Published by UnilX Education
books@unilxeducation.com
USA +1 619 798 6274
MEX +52 6631030487

MyEnglishGameZone®, 2021 ©UnilX LLC, 2021

All rights reserved. No part of this publication may be reproduced, stored in a retrieval system, or transmitted in any form or by any means, electronic, mechanical, photocopying, recording, or otherwise, without the prior permission of the copyright owner.

First Published 2021

Author: Patricia Armida Ávila Delfín
Main Characters: My English Game Zone®
Cover and Complimentary Graphics: UnilX, Innovalingua Design Team and Freepik.com
Illustration, Design and Animation Leader: Rafael Orellana
Proofreader: Sandra Rojas
Editorial Design: UNIGRÁPHICA
      Rogelio Núñez Osuna
      José Chairez Parda
      Siham Núñez Osuna
      Julieta García García

PROGRAM SYNOPSIS

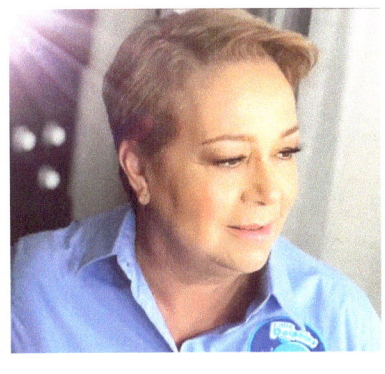

The fundamental objective of Smart Dolphin Zone is learning to communicate through interaction in the target language. The Theory of Language learning tells us that "language is a tool for communication and that students learn a language by using it to communicate."

You will find that Smart Dolphin Zone is a series based on guided everyday communicative interaction. E.g. when students are faced with real life dialogs to find out the schedule of the week's exams or to describe a classmate by his/her physical appearance, among many other authentic situations. Guided dialogs provide opportunities for language learners to interact with each other or with native speakers while feeling comfortable doing so.

This series also acknowledges the role of grammar as that of great importance for our learners to reach higher levels of proficiency and introduces the basic structures from the start of the program.

Smart Dolphin Zone also makes extensive use of authentic texts like: songs, jokes, rhymes, tongue twisters and popular children's stories. They will enrich the knowledge of culture through language.

As you can see, Smart Dolphin Zone has a solid base on the most important methodologies necessary to enhance the learning of the second language in a **dynamic** and **fun** way.

Patricia Avila Delfín

METHODOLOGIES

Vocabulary Learning

Vocabulary learning is central to language acquisition.

Specialists emphasize the need for a systematic and principled approach of vocabulary by the teacher and the learner. Teaching techniques and activities state that new words should not be learned by simple rote memorization.

It is important that new vocabulary items be presented in contexts rich enough to provide clues to meaning and that students be given multiple exposure to items they should learn.

Communicative Language Learning

Learning to communicate through interaction in the target language is the principal characteristic of the *Communicative Language Teaching* approach.

The *Theory of Language Learning* states that:
- Language is a tool for communication
- Students learn a language by using it to communicate

Integrated Skills Approach

The four basic skills in language teaching are: listening, speaking, reading, writing.

When we acquire a second language in a natural way the skills appear in that same order.

But why should we integrate the four skills when teaching the second language? If we are focused on teaching a realistic communication competence, the four skills must be developed in an integrated way.

Integrating the skills allows us to use more variety in the lessons because the range of activities will be ampler.

Spiral Learning

Learning should work like a game in a spiral, that gets a child interested while repeating and gradually increasing difficulty. It also gives students challenging activities and at the same time adds new skills.

The steps to achieve Spiral Learning are:
- Introduce new language. Move forward.
- Recap the important language learned so far.
- Add more language.
- Recap selected language: recent and earlier.
- Repeat the process.

Topic Based Approach

Topic based approach is student-centered. It helps with students' attention span.

It will hold students' interest from the start to the end of the lesson.

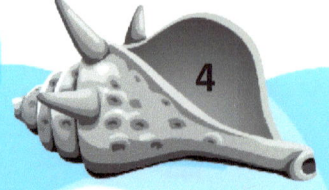

COURSE STRUCTURE

Book number	CEFR	LEVELS (12)	NUMBER OF UNITS (180)	NUMBER OF LESSONS (900)
1	Pre- A1	1	15	75
		2	15	75
2	A1.1	3	15	75
	A1.2	4	15	75
3	A2.1	5	15	75
		6	15	75
4	A2.2	7	15	75
		8	15	75
5	B1.1	9	15	75
	B1.2	10	15	75
6	B1.3	11	15	75
	B1+	12	15	75

SERIES FEATURES

- Each book with 30 units.
- Two different levels in each book.
- Each unit has five lessons:

Lesson 1: Vocabulary
In this first lesson the vocabulary that will be used during the rest of the unit will be presented through clear images that represent each word.

Lesson 2: Dialogs
The dialogs will recap the vocabulary items from lesson one and use them in everyday real situations.

Lesson 3: Reading
The reading texts will go from original stories that take the ideas of the dialogs and complete them in a text to popular stories from children's literature.

Lesson 4: Writing
Prompted writing is used in the lower levels. It encourages students to use their imagination to come up with new and creative ideas for the text. In the higher levels, students will be asked to arrange the paragraphs or the missing sentences to complete the stories they read before.

Lesson 5: Language in Use
The last part of each unit, recaps the grammar structures seen, through the presentation of language in use of the four lessons before it. There are activities that will evaluate the knowledge acquired.

CONTENTS MAP

LEVEL CEFR	UNIT	TOPIC	VOCABULARY	LANGUAGE IN USE	CAN DO STATEMENTS
5 A2.1	1	Let's learn about school activities!	School Rooms School Activities	Present progressive Affirmative, Interrogative Negative, Wh- questions	I can use simple everyday forms of greetings and address. I can participate in conversations with my friends about our school in short sentences.
	2	Let's learn about every day activities!	Every Day Activities	Present simple Affirmative, Interrogative, Negative, Wh-questions	I can ask and answer simple questions about my daily routine. I can talk about my daily activities.
	3	Let's learn about leisure activities!	Family Members Leisure Activities	Future- BE+ going to Affirmative, Interrogative Negative, Wh - questions	I can talk about my weekly plan in simple sentences.
	4	Let's learn about clothes!	Clothes Colors	Future- WILL Affirmative, Interrogative Negative, Wh-questions ***Tongue Twister Time "Betty Botter"	I can describe my clothing in simple sentences.
	5	Let's learn about feelings!	Feelings/ Emotions	Verb BE Simple past tense Affirmative	I can greet a person, inquire about his health and give polite answers to similar questions.
	6	Let's learn about community helpers!	Community Helpers Adjectives	Verb BE Simple past tense Interrogative	I can ask questions about the jobs that people do to help us.
	7	Let's learn about the city!	City Buildings	Verb BE Simple past tense Negative	I can ask about the buildings and activities in my area.
	8	Let's learn about buildings!	City Buildings Time Expressions	Verb BE Simple past tense short answers **Tongue Twister Time "Fuzzy Wuzzy"	I can reply to questions about the public buildings in my neighborhood.
	9	Let's learn about food!	Food in the Kitchen	There was/ There were Affirmative Count nouns/non-count nouns	I can understand when someone speaks to me about familiar food and drinks in simple sentences.
	10	Let's learn about festivities!	Months of the Year Festivities (Holidays)	There was/ There were Interrogative	I can talk to my friends about festivals and celebrations
	11	Let's learn about hobbies!	Hobbies	Past Progressive tense Affirmative	I can talk about my hobbies and my friends' hobbies.
	12	Let's learn about leisure activities!	Leisure Time Activities	Past Progressive tense Negative	I can understand when someone speaks in simple sentences about a familiar free-time activity.
	13	Let's learn about hobbies at home!	Rooms At Home	Past Progressive tense Interrogative Short affirmative answer	I can answer questions about my favorite hobby.
	14	Let's learn about sports!	Sports	Past Progressive tense Interrogative Short negative answer	I can handle a short simple dialog with my friends on topics of personal interest.
	15	Let's learn about more hobbies!	Hobbies Places	Past Progressive tense Wh-questions	I can ask my conversation partner what he/she does in his/her leisure time and answer the same type of questions when asked.

CONTENTS MAP

LEVEL CEFR	UNIT	TOPIC	Vocabulary	LANGUAGE IN USE	CAN DO STATEMENTS
6 A2.1	1 / 16	Let's learn about verbs!	Verbs-Past Tense +ed	Simple Past Tense Regular Verbs Affirmative ed= "T" Sound *Tongue Twister Time:* *"Peter Piper"*	I can understand when someone speaks on common topics.
	2 / 17	Let's learn about action words!	Verbs-Past Tense + ed	Simple Past Tense Regular Verbs Affirmative ed="D" Sound	I can talk about what I did yesterday, last weekend, or on vacation.
	3 / 18	Let's learn about plants and flowers!	Verbs Past Tense +ed Plants And Flowers	Simple Past Tense Regular Verbs Affirmative ed= "Ed" Sound	I can ask and answer questions about familiar plants and animals. I can describe a plant in simple sentences.
	4 / 19	Let's learn about school activities!	Verbs-School Activities	Simple Past Tense Regular Verbs Interrogative	I can easily understand simple routine tasks in the classroom.
	5 / 20	Let's learn about actions words!	Verbs In The Past Tense +ed	Simple Past Tense Regular Verbs, Interrogative *Tongue Twister Time:* *"I Wish To Wish"*	I can understand when someone speaks on common topics if the speech is slow and clear.
	6 / 21	Let's learn about sports!	Sports Past Tense Verbs + ed	Simple Past Tense Regular Verbs Short Answers	I can ask questions about everyday topics (sports) and answer similar questions.
	7 / 22	Let's learn about hobbies!	Hobbies Adjectives	Simple Past Tense Regular Verbs Wh-Questions	I can answer personal questions in simple sentences about my favorite activity.
	8 / 23	Let's learn about languages!	Countries Languages	Simple Past Tense Irregular Verbs Affirmative	I can talk to my friends about different countries. I can talk to my schoolmates about people from different countries.
	9 / 24	Let's learn about the past!	Verbs Agent Nouns	Simple Past Tense Irregular Verbs, Affirmative Agent Nouns *Tongue Twister Time:* *"Swan Swim"*	I can understand when my friend speaks about his/her family or friends.
	10 / 25	Let's learn about city!	Verbs Prepositions City Buildings	Simple Past Tense Irregular Verbs, Interrogative Prepositions	I can answer questions about places I have visited and what I did there.
	11 / 26	Let's learn about food!	Verbs Food	Simple Past Tense Irregular Verbs Negative	I can understand when someone talks to me about familiar food and drinks. I can buy something to eat or drink.
	12 / 27	Let's learn about animals!	Verbs Animals	Simple Past Tense Irregular Verbs Short Answers	I can answer questions about animals. I can tell my teacher and class about animals I have seen or kept as pets.
	13 / 28	Let's learn about actions!	Verbs	Simple Past Tense Irregular Verbs Wh- Questions *Tongue Twister Time:* *"How Many Cookies"*	I can tell my parents about what I did at school. I can describe my school activities.
	14 / 29	Let's learn about hobbies!	Hobbies	Could-Couldn't Affirmative, Interrogative, Negative	I can distinguish the tense forms, and understand when people speak about the present or past
	15 / 30	Let's learn about polite expressions!	Class Activities	Would, Affirmative, Interrogative	I can make and respond to suggestions, requests and apologies.

Level FIVE Unit ONE
Let's learn about school activities!

Learn the school rooms and the school activities

classroom — writing
computer room — working
restroom — washing

school yard — playing
library — reading

1.2 Dialogs

Level FIVE Unit ONE
Let's learn about school activities!

Practice the dialogs

Good morning!
-Good morning Miss!
How are you today?
-Fine thank you.
What's your name?
-My name is Andy.
How old are you?
-I'm 9 years old.
Where are you now?
-I'm in the classroom.
What are you doing?
-I'm writing sentences.
Thank you, have a great day.

Good morning!
-Good morning Miss!
How are you today?
-Fine thank you.
What's your name?
-My name is Sandy.
How old are you?
-I'm 8 years old.
Where are you now?
-I'm in the restroom.
What are you doing?
-I'm washing my hands.
Thank you, have a great day.

Good morning!
-Good morning Miss!
How are you today?
-Fine thank you.
What's your name?
-My name is Lucy.
How old are you?
-I'm 8 years old.
Where are you now?
-I'm in the school yard.
What are you doing?
-I'm playing volleyball.
Thank you, have a great day.

Good morning!
-Good morning Miss!
How are you today?
-Fine thank you.
What's your name?
-My name is Tony.
How old are you?
-I'm 9 years old.
Where are you now?
-I'm in the library.
What are you doing?
-I'm reading a book.
Thank you, have a great day.

Now you!

Good morning!
-Good morning, Miss!
How are you today?
-Fine, thank you.
What's your name?
-My name is _____.
How old are you?
-I'm _____ years old.
Where are you now?
-I'm in the _____.
What are you doing?
-I'm _____.
Thank you, have a great day!

Level FIVE Unit ONE
Let's learn about school activities!

1.3 Reading

 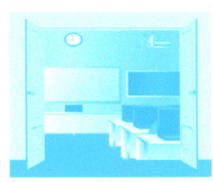  

My school

Today is a very exciting day at my school. It is first day of class. All my friends and I are very happy. Miss Patty is talking to each one of us. She is talking to Andy first. He is nine years old this year; he is in the classroom, he is writing sentences in his notebook. It is Lucy's turn. She is eight years old; she's in the school yard, she is playing volleyball. Then Miss Patty is talking to Tony. He is nine years old; he is in the library, he is reading a book. Miss Patty is talking to Harry now. He is nine years old; he is in the computer room, he is working on the computer. And finally she is talking to me. I'm Sandy, I'm eight years old; I am in the restroom, I am washing my hands, and, of course, I am talking to Miss Patty too. It is a great first day of class!
How is your first day of class?

Based on the reading complete the sentences

Andy is _____.   a) playing
Lucy is _____.   b) reading
Tony is _____.   c) washing
Harry is _____.   d) working
I am _____.   e) writing

Choose the correct school room to complete the sentence

1. Andy is writing in the _____.
   ❏ school yard   ❏ classroom   ❏ library
2. Lucy is playing in the _____.
   ❏ library   ❏ restroom   ❏ school yard
3. Tony is reading a book in the _____.
   ❏ restroom   ❏ school yard   ❏ library
4. Harry is working in the _____.
   ❏ clasroom   ❏ computer room   ❏ library
5. I am washing my hands in the _____.
   ❏ restroom   ❏ classroom   ❏ school yard

1.4 Writing

Level FIVE Unit ONE
Let's learn about school activities!

Complete the reading with words from the boxes below. Be sure to use from the correct box number. Then read.

My school

Today is a very exciting day at school.
All my friends and I are very happy.
Miss Patty is talking to each one of us. She is talking to Andy first.
He is nine years old this year; he is in the
1) _____, he is 2) _____.
It is Lucy's turn. She is eight years old, she is in the
1) _____, she is 2) _____.
Then Miss Patty is talking to Tony. He is nine years old; he is in the
1) _____, he is 2) _____.
Miss Patty is talking to Harry now. He is nine years old; he is in the
1) _____, he is 2) _____.
And finally she is talking to me. I am Sandy, I am eight years old; I am in the 1) _____, I am 2) _____
and I'm talking to Miss Patty too.
It is a great first day of class?
I am _____ years old. I am in the _____
I am _____.

1)
classroom • restroom • school yard • library
computer room

2)
writing sentences • washing hands • playing volleyball
reading a book • working

Level FIVE Unit ONE
Let's learn about school activities!

1.5 Language in use

Present progresive tense.
We use the present progressive tense to express something that is happening at this moment; something that is in progress.

Affirmative
Subject + BE + verb-ing + complement
Negative
Subjet + BE + not + verb-ing + complement
Interrogative
BE + Subject + verb-ing + complement?
Wh questions
WH + BE + Subject + verb-ing + complement?

Unscramble the sentences

1. _____ _____ _____ _____ _____?
Andy / classroom / is / in the / writing

2. _____ _____ _____ _____ _____
Harry / isn't / in the / working computer room

3. _____ _____ _____ _____?
What / doing / Tony / is

4. _____ _____ _____ _____ _____
school yard / Lucy / playing / is / in the

Choose the correct sentence

1. Which is correct?
   · Sandy is play volleyball.
   · Sandy is playing volleyball.

2. Which is correct?
   · Tony is reading a book.
   · Tony reading a book.

3. Which is correct?
   · Andy not writing a sentence.
   · Andy is not writing a sentence.

4. Which is correct?
   · Is Lucy playing volleyball?
   · Lucy is playing volleyball?

5. Which is correct?
   · What are you doing?
   · What you are doing?

How well did you do in this unit?
Write the CAN DO statement and assess yourself.
Write 3, 2, or 1
3 = VERY WELL
2 = WELL
1 = NOT SO WELL

I CAN...
_____
_____
_____
_____
_____
_____

Level FIVE Unit TWO
Let's learn about every day activities!

2.1 Vocabulary

Learn the every day activities

go to sleep
9:15

get up
7:00

take a shower
7:40

have breakfast
7:15

eat dinner
6:30

go to school
8:00

do homework
5:40

play in the yard
4:00

go home
2:20

eat lunch
9:45

15

2.2 Dialogs

Level FIVE Unit TWO
Let's learn about every day activities!

Practice the dialogs

What time do you get up every day?
- I get up at 7 o'clock every day.
Do you get up at 7:00 o'clock too?
-No, I don't. I get up at 7:15.

7:00

What time do you have breakfast every day?
- I get breakfast at 7:15.
Do you have breakfast at 7:15 too?
-No, I don't. I have breakfast at 7:25.

7:15

What time do you go to sleep?
- I go to sleep at 9:15 o'clock.
Do you go to sleep at 9:15 too?
-No, I don't. I go to sleep at 9:25.

9:15

What time do you play after school?
- I play at 4:00 o'clock.
Do you play at 4:00 too?
-No, I don't. I play at 4:30.

4:00

What time do you do your homework?
- I do my homework at 5:40.
Do you do your homework at 5:40 too?
-No, I don't. I do my homework at 6:00 o'clock.

5:40

What time do you _____ ?
- I _____ at _____ .
Do you _____ too ?
- No, I don't. I _____ at _____ .

Now you!

Level FIVE Unit TWO
Let's learn about every day activities!

2.3 Reading

Always the same

Every day I have the same routine. Always the same!
My friends do too.
For example; I get up at 7:00 and my friend Lucy gets up at 7:15.
Then I have breakfast at 7:15 but my friend has breakfast at 7:25.
I got to school at 8:00, I eat lunch at 9:45, and I go home at 2:20.
I play in the yard at 4:00 but Andy plays at 4:30.
I do my homework at 5:40 and Harry does his homework at 6:00.
I eat dinner at 6:20 and I take a shower at 7:30.
When the day ends, I go to sleep at 9:00; but my friend Tom
goes to sleep at 9:25.
Always the same. Are your days always the same?

Read carefully and then answer true or false

1. I get up at 7:15 every day.	☐ True	☐ False
2. Lucy gets up at 7:00 every day.	☐ True	☐ False
3. I play in the yard at 4:00 o'clock.	☐ True	☐ False
4. I do my homework at 5:40 every day.	☐ True	☐ False
5. Harry does his homework at 5:00.	☐ True	☐ False
6. I go to sleep at 9:30 o'clock.	☐ True	☐ False
7. Tom goes to sleep at 9:25.	☐ True	☐ False

2.4 Writing

Complete the reading with the names of your friends and the times that are true for you and your friends

Always the same

Every day I have the same routine. Always the same! My friends do too.
For example; I get up at _____ and my friend gets up at _____.
Then I have breakfast at _____ but my friend has breakfast at _____. I got to school at _____, I eat lunch at _____, and I go home at _____.
I play at the yard at _____ but my friend _____ does homework at _____. I eat dinner at _____ and I take a shower at _____.
When the day ends, I go to sleep at _____; but my friend _____ goes to sleep at _____.
Always the same. Are your days always the same?

Level FIVE Unit TWO
Let's learn about every day activities!

2.5 Language in use

> We use the Present Simple Tense to express every day activities, routines and habits.
>
> **Affirmative**
> Subject + verb + complement
> **Negative**
> Subject + do/does + not (don't-doesn't) + verb + complement
> **Interrogative**
> BE + Subject + verb-ing + complement?
> **Wh questions**
> Do/does + Subject + verb + complement?

Circle the correct clock

1) Quarter after seven.
   7:00   **7:15**

2) Twenty before ten.
   9:20   **9:40**

3) Ten after eleven.
   11:10   10:11

4) Four fifteen.
   4:50   **4:15**

5) Six thirty five.
   6:35   6:53

Choose the correct sentence

1. Which is correct?
   - I get up at 7:00.
   - I gets up at 7:00.

2. Which is correct?
   - He eat lunch at 11:00.
   - He eats lunch at 11:00.

3. Which is correct?
   - Does he play in the yard?
   - Does he plays in the yard?

4. Which is correct?
   - I don't go to school.
   - I doesn't go to school.

5. Which is correct?
   - He don't read a book.
   - He doesn't read a book.

How well did you do in this unit?
Write the CAN DO statement and assess yourself.
Write 3, 2, or 1
3 = VERY WELL
2 = WELL
1 = NOT SO WELL

I CAN...
_____
_____
_____
_____
_____
_____

Level FIVE Unit THREE
Let's learn about leisure activities!

3.1
Vocabulary

Learn the leisure activities

21

3.2 Dialogs

Level FIVE Unit THREE
Let's learn about leisure activities!

Practice the dialogs

What is your father going to do on Sunday?
-He is going to fish. He always goes fishing on Sunday.

What is your mother going to do on Monday?
-She is going to jog. She always goes jogging on Monday.

What is your brother going to do on Thursday?
-He is going to swim. He always goes swimming on Thursday.

What is your sister going to do on Wednesday?
-She is going to skate. She always goes skating on Wednesday.

What are you going to do on Friday?
-I am going to rock-climb. I always go rock-climbing on Friday.

What are you and your family going to do on Saturday.
We are going to hike. We always go hiking on Saturday.

What are you going to do on _____?
- I am going to _____.
I always go _____ on _____.

Level FIVE Unit THREE
Let's learn about leisure activities!

3.3 Reading

What are we going to do?

My family and I love to keep busy with healthy activities all through the week. Do you want to know what we are going to do? Well, just read ahead!
My father is going to fish on Sunday. He always goes fishing on Sunday; he says it is relaxing. My mother is going to jog in the park; she always goes jogging with her friends on Monday. My sister is going to skate on Wednesday. She is in the skating team at school and Wednesday is when they practice together. My brother is going to swim in the pool on Thursday; he goes every Thursday afternoon. He wants to become a world class swimmer! I always go rock-climbing on Friday;
I am going to go this Friday too.
Rock-climbing is great! My family and I go hiking together every Saturday; this Saturday the weather is going to be perfect for hiking! Do you like my family´s activities?
What are you going to do this week?

Answer the questions

1. Who is going to fish on Sunday?
   _____
2. Who is going to swim on Thursday?
   _____
3. Who is going to skate on Wednesday?
   _____
4. Who is going to climb on Friday?
   _____
5. Who is going to hike on Saturday?
   _____
6. Who is going to jog on Monday?
   _____

Circle the correct answer

1. What is mother going to do on Monday?
   hike   fish   jog

2. When is father going to fish?
   Sunday   Monday   Tuesday

3. What is brother going to do on Thursday?
   swim   rock-climb   skate

4. What is sister going to do on Wednesday?
   rock - climb   swim   skate

3.4 Writing

Level FIVE Unit THREE
Let's learn about leisure activities!

Complete the reading with the names of your friends or family and the days for the activities from the box below

What are we going to do?

My family and I love to keep busy with healthy activities all through the week. Do you want to know what we are going to do? Well, just read ahead!

My _____ is going to fish on _____. He/She always goes fishing on _____; it is relaxing. My _____ is going to jog in the park; he/she always goes jogging with her friends on _____. My _____ is going to skate on _____. He/She is in the skating team at school and _____ is when they practice together. My _____ is going to swim in the pool on _____; he/she goes every _____ afternoon. He/She wants to become a world class swimmer! _____ always go rock-climbing on _____; _____ am going to go this _____ too. Rock climbing is great! My family and I go hiking together every Saturday; this Saturday the weather is going to be perfect for hiking!

Do you like my family's activities?
What are you going to do this week?

Sunday / Monday / Tuesday / Wednesday / Thursday / Friday / Saturday

Level FIVE Unit THREE
Let's learn about leisure activities!

FUTURE TENSE
to express a planned action in the future we use
BE + going to + verb

Affirmative
Subject + BE + going to + verb
Negative
Subjet + BE NOT + going to + verb
Interrogative
BE + Subject + going to + verb?
Wh questions
Wh-q + BE + Subject + going to + verb?

Unscramble the sentences

1. ____ ____ ____ ____ ____ .
   skate / to / she / is / going

2. ____ ____ ____ ____ ____ .
   isn't / swim / to / going / he

3. ____ ____ ____ ____ ____ .
   I / rock-climb / going / am / to

4. ____ ____ ____ ____ ____ ?
   hike / you / going / are / to

5. ____ ____ ____ ____ ____ ____ ?
   Are / going / do / what / they / to

Choose the correct sentence

1. Which is correct?
   · We are going to fishing.
   · We are going to fish.

2. Which is correct?
   · You are going to swim?
   · Are you going to swim?

3. Which is correct?
   · He is not going to jog.
   · He is going not to jog.

4. Which is correct?
   · What are you going to do?
   · What you are going to do?

How well did you do in this unit?

Write the CAN DO statement and assess yourself.

Write 3, 2, or 1

3 = VERY WELL

2 = WELL

1 = NOT SO WELL

I CAN...

_____

_____

_____

_____

_____

_____

Level FIVE Unit FOUR
Let's learn about clothes!

4.1 Vocabulary

Learn the names of the clothes

blue

jeans

black

shoes

red

T-shirt

brown

jacket

white

socks

W	B	F	B	S	T	J	E	B	I
N	L	L	K	S	D	X	T	R	K
E	U	C	H	S	X	A	I	O	G
E	O	I	O	S	H	N	H	W	A
S	R	Q	E	P	N	O	W	N	K
T	F	T	E	V	N	A	E	D	C
Z	K	M	G	I	L	R	E	S	F
B	Q	T	E	K	C	A	J	J	C
E	Q	P	N	F	D	T	I	I	H
B	L	A	C	K	D	E	T	T	Z

RED
BLUE
WHITE
BLACK
BROWN
T-SHIRT
JEANS
SOCKS
SHOES
JACKET

4.2 Dialogs

Level FIVE Unit FOUR
Let's learn about clothes!

Practice the dialogs

What will you wear tomorrow?
-I think I will wear my brown jacket.
I certainly won't wear my red jacket.
-Great!

What will you wear tomorrow?
-I think I will wear my black shoes.
I certainly won't wear my blue shoes.
-Great!

What will you wear tomorrow?
-I think I will wear my red T-shirt.
I certainly won't wear my brown T-shirt.
-Great!

What will you wear tomorrow?
-I think I will wear my blue jeans.
I certainly won't wear my white jeans.
-Great!

What will you wear tomorrow?
-I think I will wear my white socks.
I certainly won't wear my brown socks.
-Great!

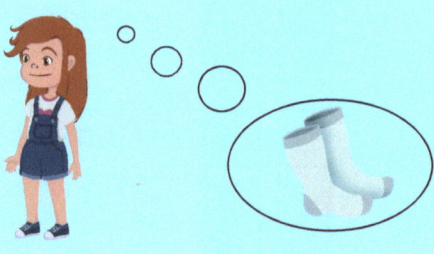

Now you!

What will you wear tomorrow?
- I think I will wear my _____.
I certainly won't wear my _____.
-Great!

Level FIVE Unit FOUR
Let's learn about clothes!

What will you wear?

There is going to be a big party at school tomorrow. And I want to know what everybody is going to wear.
What will Andy wear? He thinks he will wear a red T-shirt; he is sure he won't wear a brown T-shirt. What will Sandy wear? She says she will wear white socks; she won't wear brown socks.
What will Tony wear? He thinks he will wear black shoes; he is sure he won't wear blue shoes. Lucy will wear blue jeans, she is sure she won't wear white jeans.
The party is going to be fun and everybody is going to look great!
What will you wear to the party?

Who will wear...?

Who will wear a red T-shirt?
- ❏ Lucy
- ❏ Andy
- ❏ Tony

Who will wear white socks?
- ❏ Sandy
- ❏ Lucy
- ❏ Andy

Who will wear black shoes?
- ❏ Sandy
- ❏ Andy
- ❏ Tony

Who will wear blue jeans?
- ❏ Lucy
- ❏ Andy
- ❏ Sandy

Answer true or false according to the reading

Andy will wear a brown T-shirt.
- ❏ True   ❏ False

Sandy will wear brown socks.
- ❏ True   ❏ False

Tony will wear black shoes.
- ❏ True   ❏ False

Lucy will wear white jeans.
- ❏ True   ❏ False

4.4 Writing

Level FIVE Unit FOUR
Let's learn about clothes!

Complete the reading with the words from the box below

What will you wear?

There is going to be a big party at school tomorrow.
And I want to know what everybody is going to wear.
What will Andy wear? He thinks he will wear a _____;
he is sure he won't wear a _____. What will Sandy wear?
She says she will wear _____; she won't wear _____.
What will Tony wear? He thinks he will wear _____;
he is sure he won't wear _____. Lucy will wear _____.
She is sure she won't wear _____.
The party is going to be fun and everybody is going to look great!
What will you wear to the party?

---

red T-shirt • white socks • black shoes • blue jeans
brown T-shirt • brown socks • blue shoes • white jeans

Level FIVE Unit FOUR
Let's learn about clothes!

4.5 Language in use

FUTURE TENSE WILL
We use WILL to express future events and when we think or believe something about the future.

Affirmative
Subject + WILL + verb + complement.
Negative
Subject + WILL-NOT (won't) + verb + complement.
Interrogative
WILL + Subject + verb + complement?
Wh questions
Subject + WILL-NOT (won't) + verb + complement?

Unscramble the sentences

1. _____ .
   jacket / brown / my / wear / will / I

2. _____ .
   won't / blue / she / jeans / wear

3. _____ ?
   wear / who / white / socks / will

4. _____ ?
   tomorrow / you / wear / what / will

5. _____ .
   wear / will / a red / T-shirt / I

Tongue Twister Time

Betty Botter bought
a bit of better butter.
But the bit of better butter
Betty Botter bought,
was a bit bitter for better butter.

31

How well did you do in this unit?
Write the CAN DO statement and assess yourself.
Write 3, 2, or 1
3 = VERY WELL
2 = WELL
1 = NOT SO WELL

I CAN...
_____
_____
_____
_____
_____
_____

Level FIVE Unit FIVE
Let's learn about feelings!

5.1 Vocabulary

Learn the feelings

sick	tired	sad	hungry

angry	scared

thirsty	nervous	cold	bored

5.2 Dialogs

Level FIVE Unit FIVE
Let's learn about feelings!

Practice the dialogs

Hello Sandy, how are you today?
-Hi Tony! Today? Not so bad. But yesterday...
Yesterday?
-Yes, I was sick and cold yesterday.
I'm sorry to hear that!
-Thank you.

Hello Andy, how are you today?
-Hi Sandy! Today? Not so bad. But yesterday...
Yesterday?
-Yes, I was sad and angry yesterday.
I'm sorry to hear that!
-Thank you.

Hello Harry, how are you today?
-Hi Sandy! Today? Not so bad. But yesterday...
Yesterday?
-Yes, I was scared and nervous yesterday.
I'm so sorry to hear that!
-Thank you.

Hello Lucy, how are you today?
-Hi Andy! Today? Not so bad. But yesterday...
Yesterday?
-Yes, I was bored and tired yesterday.
I'm sorry to hear that!
-Thank you.

Hello Tony, how are you today?
-Hi Sandy! Today? Not so bad. But yesterday...
Yesterday?
-Yes, I was hungry and thirsty yesterday.
I'm so sorry to hear that!
-Thank you.

Hello, how are you today?
-Hi, Today? Not so bad... But yesterday
Yesterday?
-Yes, I was _____ and _____ yesterday.
I'm sorry to hear that.
-Thank you.

Level FIVE Unit FIVE
Let's learn about feelings!

5.3 Reading

How were you yesterday?

Yesterday was a difficult day. My friends and I were feeling strange not the same as usual.

Sandy was cold but she also was sick yesterday; she was in bed with her blankets all day. Lucy was tired but she was also bored; her TV was broken.

Then Tony was thirsty and he was very hungry; well he is always very hungry.

Andy was sad because he lost his tablet and then he was angry because his tablet was in his brother's room. Harry was scared but he was very nervous during an exam.

Yes, it certainly was a difficult day for all my friends yesterday. The good thing about it is that today we are all feeling great! How are you today? How were you yesterday?

According to reading choose the correct answer

1. How was Andy?
   ☐ sick and cold
   ☐ sad and angry
   ☐ scared and nervous
2. How was Sandy?
   ☐ tired and bored
   ☐ hungry and thirsty
   ☐ sick and cold
3. How was Lucy?
   ☐ tired and bored
   ☐ sick and cold
   ☐ scared and nervous
4. How was Tony?
   ☐ tired and bored
   ☐ sad and angry
   ☐ hungry and thirsty
5. How was Harry?
   ☐ scared and nervous
   ☐ sand and angry
   ☐ sick and cold

Read again and then complete the sentences

1. Sandy was ____ and ____ yesterday.

2. Lucy was ____ and ____ yesterday.

3. Tony was ____ and ____ yesterday.

4. Andy was ____ and ____ yesterday.

5. Harry was ____ and ____ yesterday.

5.4 Writing

Level FIVE Unit FIVE
Let's learn about feelings!

Choose a word and fill in a blank. You can use several times each word. Then read aloud.

How were you yesterday?

Yesterday was a difficult day. My friends and I were feeling strange not the same as usual.
Sandy was _____ but she also was _____ yesterday.
Lucy was _____ but she was also _____; her TV was broken.
Then Tony was _____ and he was very _____.
Andy was _____ because he lost his tablet and then he was _____ because his tablet was in his brother's room. Harry was _____ but he was very _____ during an exam.
Yes, it certainly was a difficult day for all my friends yesterday. The good thing about it is that today we are all feeling great!
How are you today?
How were you yesterday? I was _____ and _____.

---

angry · bored · cold · hungry · nervous · sad
scared · sick · thirsty · tired

Level FIVE Unit FIVE
Let's learn about feelings!

5.5 Language in use

The verb BE is an irregular verb in Simple Past.
There are two simple past forms on the verb BE; was/were
We use was with I/he/she/it.
We use were with we/you/ they

Affirmative
I was tired yesterday.
You were scared yesterday.
Sandy was sick yesterday.
My friends were hungry.

Label the feelings

_____ _____ _____ _____

_____ _____ _____ _____

Choose the correct form of the verb BE past tense

1. Sandy _____ cold yesterday.
   a) was   b) were

2. Lucy and Tony _____ tired yesterday.
   a) was   b) were

3. I _____ hungry yesterday.
   a) was   b) were

4. Andy and I _____ angry yesterday.
   a) was   b) were

5. Harry _____ nervous yesterday.
   a) was   b) were

6. You _____ sick yesterday.
   a) was   b) were

7. You and Tom _____ bored yesterday.
   a) was   b) were

How well did you do in this unit?

Write the CAN DO statement and assess yourself.

Write 3, 2, or 1

3 = VERY WELL

2 = WELL

1 = NOT SO WELL

I CAN...

_____
_____
_____
_____
_____
_____
_____

Level FIVE Unit SIX
Let's learn about community helpers!

6.1
Vocabulary

Learn the community helpers

police officer

doctor

dentist

firefighter

teacher

39

6.2 Dialogs

Level FIVE Unit SIX
Let's learn about community helpers!

Practice the dialogs

Was your father a police officer?
-Yes, he was. He was a brave police officer.
Cool!

Was your mother a doctor?
-Yes, She was. She was an excellent doctor.
Cool!

Was your father a doctor?
-Yes, he was. He was an excellent doctor.
Cool!

Were your mom and dad dentists?
-Yes, they were. They were friendly dentists.
Cool!

Were you and dad teachers?
-Yes, we were. We were incredible teachers.
Cool!

Was your _____ a _____?
-Yes, _____ _____. _____ was an _____ _____.
Cool!

Level FIVE Unit SIX
Let's learn about community helpers!

6.3 Reading

Photos...

Miss Patty asked us to bring photos of people that we admire from our family. All my friends and I have great people to talk about. Just see!

Lucy's grandma was an excellent doctor; she is retired now. She lives in Miami.

Tony's grandma and grandpa both were dentists. They were very friendly. They are now traveling around the world.

Andy's parents were teachers; they were incredible. They are now working in an office. Harry's father was a firefighter; he was wonderful! Now he is teaching future firefighters.

And I am so proud to say, my grandma was a police officer; she was so brave! Now she lives with us.

Everybody was so cool, right?
Who do you admire in your family, do you have photos?

According to reading choose true or false

1. Sandy's grandma was a police officer?
   ☐ true   ☐ false
2. Lucy's grandpa was a firefighter.
   ☐ true   ☐ false
3. Tony's grandparents were dentists.
   ☐ true   ☐ false
4. Andy's parents were doctors.
   ☐ true   ☐ false
5. Harry's father was teacher.
   ☐ true   ☐ false

Read again and then complete the answers.

1. Was your mother a police officer?
   Yes, _____ _____. She was a _____ police officer.
2. Was your father a doctor?
   Yes, _____ _____. He was a _____ doctor.
3. Were your mom and dad dentists?
   Yes, _____ _____. They were _____ dentists.
4. Were you and dad teachers?
   Yes, _____ _____. We were _____ teachers.
5. Were you a firefighter?
   Yes, _____ _____. I was a _____ firefighter.

6.4 Writing

Level FIVE Unit SIX
Let's learn about community helpers!

Choose a word and fill in a blank. You can use several times each word. Then read aloud.

Photos...

Miss Patty asked us to bring photos of people that we admire from our family. All my friends and I have great people to talk about. Just see!

Lucy's grandma was a/ an (2)_____ (1)_____; she is retired now. She lives in Miami.

Tony's grandma and grandpa both were (1)_____. They were very (2)____. They are now traveling around the world.

Andy's parents were (1)_____; they were (2)_____. They are now working in an office. Harry's father was a/an (1)_____; he was (2)_____!

And I am so proud to say, my grandma was a/an (1)_____; she was so (2)_____! Now she lives with us.

Everybody was so cool, right?
Who do you admire in your family, do you have photos?

---

1) police officer(s) / doctor(s) / firefighter(s) / teacher(s) / dentist(s)

2) excellent / friendly / wonderful / brave / incredible

Level FIVE Unit SIX
Let's learn about community helpers!

6.5
Language in use

The verb BE is an irregular verb in Simple Past.
There are two simple past forms on the verb BE: was/were
We use was with I/he/she/it.
We use were with we/you/they

Interrogative
BE + subject + complement?
Were you a doctor?
Was your mother a dentist?
Short affirmative answers:
Yes, I was.
Yes, she was.

Complete the paragraph with was or were

I _____ a brave police officer.

My friend _____ an incredible dentist.

They _____ friendly teachers.

You _____ a wonderful firefighter.

Tom _____ an excellent doctor.

We _____ all very cool.

Write the affirmative short answer

1. Were you a brave police officer?
_____, _____ _____.

2. Was Lucy's grandpa an excellent doctor?
_____, _____ _____.

3. Were Tony's grandparents friendly dentists?
_____, _____ _____.

4. Were you and dad incredible teachers?
_____, _____ _____

5. Was Harry's mother a wonderful firefighter?
_____, _____ _____.

How well did you do in this unit?
Write the CAN DO statement and assess yourself.
Write 3, 2, or 1
3 = VERY WELL
2 = WELL
1 = NOT SO WELL

I CAN...
_____
_____
_____
_____
_____
_____
_____

Level FIVE Unit SEVEN
Let's learn about the city!

7.1
Vocabulary

Learn the places in the city

7.2 Dialogs

Level FIVE Unit SEVEN
Let's learn about the city!

Practice the dialogs

Were you at the park yesterday?
-No, I wasn't at the park. I was at the mall.

Was Harry at school yesterday?
-No, he wasn't at school. He was at the library.

Was Lucy at the movie theater yesterday?
-No, she wasn't at the movie theater. She was at the restaurant.

Were Lucy and Sandy at church on Sunday?
-No, they weren't at church. They were at the airport.

Were you and Tony at the supermarket on Saturday?
No, we weren't at the supermarket. We were at the bank.

Were/were _____ at the _____ on _____?
-No, _____ weren't/wasn't at _____. We were/was at the _____.

Now you!

Level FIVE Unit SEVEN
Let's learn about the city!

7.3 Reading

Around the city

It is summer! The afternoons are so nice that my friends and I can go around visiting different places in the city. There are some places that we usually go. But this week we were at other places. Where were we?

Well… Andy wasn't at the park; he was at the mall with his mom. Lucy wasn't in the movie theater; she was in the restaurant with her cousin Nancy. It was her birthday. Harry wasn't at school; he was reading books in the library. Lucy and Sandy weren't at church on Sunday; they were at the airport. Sandy's dad was arriving from another country. Tony and I weren't at the supermarket on Saturday; we were at the bank. As you can see, we were enjoying the city during the afternoon at different places. It was a great week. Where were you in the afternoon last week?

According to the reading choose true or false

1. Andy was at the park.
   ☐ true   ☐ false
2. Lucy wasn't at the movie theater.
   ☐ true   ☐ false
3. Harry was at school.
   ☐ true   ☐ false
4. Lucy and Sandy weren't at church
   ☐ true   ☐ false
5. Tony and Lucy were at the bank.
   ☐ true   ☐ false

Read again and then complete the sentences

1. Andy wasn't at the _____; he was at the _____.

2. Lucy wasn't in the _____; she was in the _____.

3. Harry wasn't at _____; he was in the _____.

4. Lucy and Sandy weren't at _____; they were at the _____.

5. Tony and Lucy weren't at the _____; they were at the _____.

47

7.4 Writing

Level FIVE Unit SEVEN
Let's learn about the city!

Choose a phrase and fill in a blank. You can use several times each phrase. Then read aloud.

Around the city

It is summer! The afternoons are so nice that my friends and I can go around visiting different places in the city.
There are some places that we usually go.
But this week we were at other cool places. Where were we? Well…
Andy wasn't _____ as usual; he was _____ with his mom.
Lucy wasn't _____ ; she was _____ with her cousin Nancy.
It was her birthday.
Harry wasn't _____ as always; he was reading books _____ .
Lucy and Sandy weren't _____ on Sunday like always; they were _____ .
Tony and I weren't _____ on Saturday; we were _____ .
As you can see, we were enjoying the city during the afternoon at different places.
It was a great week.
Where were you in the afternoon last week?

---

at the park • at the mall • at the movie theater
at the restaurant • at school • in the library
at church • at the airport • at the supermarket
at the bank

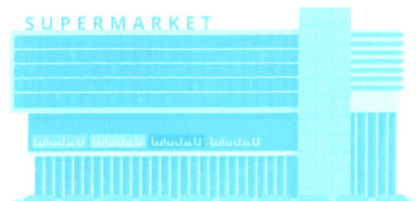

Level FIVE Unit SEVEN
Let's learn about the city!

> The verb BE is an irregular verb in Simple Past.
>
> There are two simple past forms of the verb BE: was- were.
> We use was with I/ he/she/it
> We use were with we/you/they
>
> Negative:
>
> Subject+ BE-NOT + complement.
> Andy wasn't in the park.
> They weren't at the supermarket.

Complete the negative answer

1. Were you at the park yesterday?
   No, _____ _____ at the park yesterday.

2. Was Sandy at church yesterday?
   No, _____ _____ at church yesterday.

3. Were Andy and Tony at the restaurant yesterday?
   No, _____ _____ at the restaurant yesterday.

4. Were you and Lucy at the supermarket yesterday?
   No, _____ _____ at the supermarket yesterday.

5. Was Andy at the mall yesterday?
   No, _____ _____ at the mall yesterday.

How well did you do in this unit?
Write the CAN DO statement and assess yourself.
Write 3, 2, or 1
3 = VERY WELL
2 = WELL
1 = NOT SO WELL

I CAN...
_____
_____
_____
_____
_____
_____
_____

Level FIVE Unit EIGHT
Let's learn about buildings!

8.1
Vocabulary

Learn the names of the buildings

morning

afternoon

evening

night

8.2 Dialogs

Unit EIGHT
Let's learn about buildings!

Practice the dialogs

Were you at the Fire Station yesterday morning?
-No, I wasn't. I was there yesterday afternoon.
Oh, I see!

Was Sandy at the Police Station yesterday afternoon?
-No, she wasn't. She was there yesterday morning.
Oh, I see!

Was Andy at the Dental Clinic yesterday evening?
-No, he wasn't. He was there yesterday afternoon.
Oh, I see!

Were you and Harry at the Post Office yesterday morning?
-No, we weren't. We were there last night.
Oh, I see!

Were Lucy and Tony at the Zoo yesterday afternoon?
-No, they weren't. They were there yesterday morning.
Oh, I see!

Were /Was _____ at the
_____ yesterday _____?
-No, _____ _____. _____ were/was
there yesterday _____.
Oh, I see!

Now you!

Level FIVE Unit EIGHT
Let's learn about buildings!

8.3 Reading

Visiting the city

I just moved to this beautiful city a few months ago. My friends from school were telling me about the incredible buildings there are here. So I asked them to show me around yesterday. They were all happy to do it. But it wasn't easy to meet them at the different places. In fact I wasn't there at the same time they were.
I missed them completely.

Tony was at the Fire Station in the afternoon, and I was there in the morning.
Sandy was in the Police Station in the morning and I was there in the afternoon.
Andy was at the Dental Clinic in the afternoon and I was there in the morning.
Andy and Harry were in the Post Office at night and I was there in the morning.
Lucy and Tony were at the Zoo in the morning and I was there in the afternoon.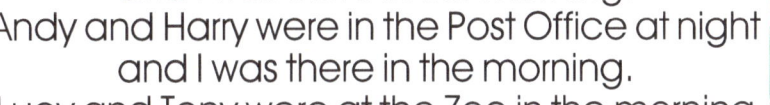
So, next time I will surely have a pencil ready and write down the times to meet my friends to visit the city with them. I don't want to miss them again!

According to the reading circle ✓ true or ✗ false

1. Sandy was at the Police Station in the morning.

2. Andy wasn't at the Dental Clinic in the afternoon.

3. Andy and Harry were at the Post Office at night.

4. Lucy and Tony weren't at the Zoo in the morning.

5. Tony was at the Fire Station in the afternoon.
   ✓ ✗

Read carefully and choose the correct response

1. Were you at the Fire Station in the morning?
   ☐ Yes, I was.   ☐ No, I wasn't.

2. Was Sandy at the Police Station in the morning?
   ☐ Yes, she was.   ☐ No, she wasn't.

3. Was Andy at the Dental Clinic in the evening?
   ☐ Yes, he was.   ☐ No, he wasn't.

4. Were Andy and Harry at the Post Office at night?
   ☐ Yes, they were.   ☐ No, they weren't.

5. Were Lucy and Tony at the Zoo in the morning?
   ☐ Yes, they were.   ☐ No, they weren't.

8.4 Writing

Unit EIGHT
Let's learn about buildings!

Choose a time expression and fill in a blank. You can use several times each time expresion. Then read aloud.

Visiting the city

I just moved to this beautiful city a few months ago.
My friends from school were telling me about the
incredible buildings there are here.
So I asked them to show me around yesterday.
They were all happy to do it. But it wasn't easy to meet them
at the different places. In fact I wasn't there at the same time they were.
I missed them completely.
Tony was at the Fire Station in the _____,
and I was there in the _____.
Sandy was in the Police Station in the _____ and I was there in the _____.
Andy was at the Dental Clinic in the _____
and I was there in the _____.
Andy and Harry were in the Post Office at _____
and I was there in the _____.
Lucy and Tony were at the Zoo in the _____
and I was there in the _____.
So, next time I will surely have a pencil ready
and write down the times to meet my friends to visit the city with them.
I don't want to miss them again!

morning • afternoon • evening • night

Level FIVE Unit EIGHT
Let's learn about buildings!

8.5 Language in use

We form the interrogative form of the Simple Past Tense of the verb BE:
BE + Subject + complement?
Was Sandy at the Police Station?

We give a short affirmative answer:
Yes, (comma) + (personal pronoun) + BE. (period)
Yes, she was.
We give the short negative answer:
No, (comma) + (personal pronoun) + BE-not. (period)
No, she wasn't.

Unscramble the sentences

1. ___ ___ ___ ___ ___ .
   in the / Sandy / was / at the Police Station / morning
2. ___ ___ ___ ___ ___ .
   Dental Clinic / in the / Andy wasn't / in the / afternoon
3. ___ ___ ___ ___ ___ .
   Andy and Harry / Post Office were / at the / at night
4. ___ ___ ___ ___ ___ .
   Zoo / in the / at the / weren't Lucy and Tony / morning
5. ___ ___ ___ ___ ___ .
   Fire Station / in the / Tony / was afternoon / at the

Tongue Twister Time

Fuzzy Wuzzy was a bear,
Fuzzy Wuzzy had no hair,
Fuzzy Wuzzy wasn't very
Fuzzy, was he?

How well did you do in this unit?
Write the CAN DO statement and assess yourself.
Write 3, 2, or 1
3 = VERY WELL
2 = WELL
1 = NOT SO WELL

I CAN...
_____
_____
_____
_____
_____
_____

Level FIVE Unit NINE
Let's learn about food!

9.1 Vocabulary

Learn the names of food

9.2 Dialogs

Level FIVE Unit NINE
Let's learn about food!

Practice the dialogs

There were some apples and some oranges here a minute ago. Where are they?
-They're on the counter.
Ok, Thanks.

There was some sugar here a minute ago. Where is it?
-It's on the table.
Ok, thanks.

There were some cookies here a minute ago. Where are they?
-They're in the cupboard.
Ok, Thanks.

There was some milk here a minute ago.
-It's in the fridge.
Ok, thanks.

There were some bananas here a minute. Where are they?
-They're on the table.
Ok, thanks.
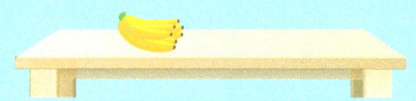

There was some juice here a minute ago. Where is it?
-It's in the fridge.
Ok, thanks.

Now you!

There were some _____ here a minute ago. Where are they?
-They're on the _____.
Ok. Thanks.

There was some _____ here a minute ago. Where is it?
-It's on the _____.
Ok. Thanks.

Level FIVE Unit NINE
Let's learn about food!

9.3 Reading

From the supermarket

There were so many delicious things to eat and drink at home today.
There were some bananas on the table. There were my favorite cookies in the cupboard. There was fresh milk in the fridge and some juice too.
On the counter there were red apples, green pears and juicy oranges.
There was my mom's favorite bread in the cupboard.
And for dad, there was some sugar and coffee on the table.
For sure my mom was in the supermarket today.
She always gets the best food for everybody at home. Thanks mom!
What is your favorite food?

According to the reading circle ✓ true and ✗ false

1. There were some oranges in the fridge. ✗ ✓
2. There were some cookies on the table. ✗ ✓
3. There was sugar in the cupboard. ✗ ✓
4. There was some juice on the table. ✗ ✓
5. There were some apples on the counter. ✗ ✓

Read carefully and complete the sentence with the words from the box at the bottom

1. There were some _____ on the table.
2. There were my favorite _____ in the cupboard.
3. There was fresh _____ and _____ in the fridge.
4. There were _____, _____ and _____ on the counter.
5. There was mom's favorite _____ in the cupboard.
6. There was _____ and _____ for dad on the table.

apples / bananas / bread / coffee / cookies / juice / milk / oranges / pears / sugar

59

9.4 Writing

Level FIVE Unit NINE
Let's learn about food!

Choose any food and fill in a blank. But be careful to choose from the correct box. You can use several times each food. Then read aloud.

> **From the supermarket**
>
> There were so many delicious things to eat and drink at home today.
> There were some (2)_____ on the table.
> There were my favorite (2) _____ in the cupboard.
> There was fresh (1) _____ in the fridge and some (1)_____ too.
> On the counter there were (2) _____, (2) _____ and (2) _____.
> There was my mom's favorite (1) _____ in the cupboard.
> And for dad, there was some (1) _____ and (1) _____ on the table.
> For sure my mom was in the supermarket today.
> She always gets the best food for everybody at home.
> Thanks mom!
> What is your favorite food?

1) bread • coffee • juice • milk • sugar

2) apples • bananas • cookies • oranges • pears

Level FIVE Unit NINE
Let's learn about food!

9.5
Language in use

> We use there was and there were in the Simple Past Tense to express that something existed.
>
> There was for singular or non-count nouns.
> There was some milk in the fridge.
>
> There were for plural or count nouns.
> There were some oranges on the counter.

Complete the sentences with the words from the box below

coffee / apples / there was / were

1. _____ were some bananas on the table.

2. There _____ cookies on the table.

3. There _____ fresh milk in the fridge.

4. There was _____ in the cupboard.

5. There were _____ for dad on the table.

Choose the sentence that is correct

1. Which is correct?
   ☐ There were some coffee
   ☐ There was some coffee.

2. Which is correct?
   ☐ There was some oranges.
   ☐ There were some oranges.

3. Which is correct?
   ☐ There were some milk.
   ☐ There was some milk.

4. Which is correct?
   ☐ There was some cookies.
   ☐ There were some cookies.

5. Which is correct?
   ☐ There was some bread.
   ☐ There were some bread.

How well did you do in this unit?

Write the CAN DO statement and assess yourself.

Write 3, 2, or 1

3 = VERY WELL

2 = WELL

1 = NOT SO WELL

I CAN...

_____

_____

_____

_____

_____

_____

Level FIVE Unit TEN
Let's learn about festivities!

10.1 Vocabulary

Learn the year's festivities

January   **February**   **March**   **April**

May   **June**   **July**   **August**

September   **October**   **November**   **December**

63

10.2 Dialogs

Practice the dialogs

Was there a Valentine's party last February?
-Yes, there was. It was fun.

Was there a Mother's Day festival last May?
-Yes, there was. It was wonderful.

Was there a Halloween dance last October?
-Yes, there was. It was fantastic.

Was there a Thanksgiving dinner last November?
-Yes, there was. It was delicious.

Was there a Christmas play last December?
-Yes, there was. It was brilliant.

Now you!

Was there a _____ last _____
-Yes, there was. It was brilliant.

Festive occasions

Today my school friends and I were remembering what we celebrated last year.

In February there was a big Valentine's Day party, it was fun; we were all happy dancing and giving each other Valentine's Day cards.

In May there was a Mother's Day festival, it was wonderful; each class prepared something special for our moms.

In October there was a Halloween dance, it was fantastic; we were all dressed up in different costumes.

In November there was a Thanksgiving dinner, it was delicious; we were all very grateful for our friends, family and food.

In December there was a Christmas play, it was brilliant; I was the donkey in the Christmas scene!

Last year was so fun. I am pretty sure this year will also be fun!

Label the festivities

_____   _____

_____   _____

_____

Read the text carefully and complete the sentences with the festivities

1. There was a _____ in May. It was wonderful.

2. There was a _____ in December. It was brilliant.

3. There was a _____ in February. It was fun.

4. There was a _____ in November. It was delicious.

5. There was a _____ in October. It was fantastic.

Valentine's Day/ Mother's Day/ Halloween/ Christmas/ Thanksgiving

10.4 Writing

Level FIVE Unit TEN
Let's learn about festivities!

Choose a month and an adjective and fill in a blank. Be careful to choose from the correct box. You can use several times each adjective. Then read aloud.

Festive occasions

Today my school friends and I were remembering what we celebrate last year.

In (1)____ there was a big Valentine's Day party, it was (2)____; we were all happy dancing and giving each other Valentine's Day cards.

In (1)____ there was a Mother's Day festival, it was (2)____; each class prepared something special for our moms.

In (1)____ there was a Halloween dance, it was (2)____; we were all dressed up in different customes.

In (1)____ there was a Thanksgiving dinner, it was (2)____; we were all very grateful for our friends, family and food.

In (1)____ there was a Christmas play, it was (2)____; I was the donkey in the Christmas scene!

Last year was so fun. I am pretty sure this year will also be fun!

1) January / February / March / April / May / June / July
August / September / October / November / December

2) fantastic / awesome / brilliant / fun / delicious / wonderful / perfect / incredible

October

Thanksgiving

Valentine's Day

August

Level FIVE Unit TEN
Let's learn about festivities!

10.5 Language in use

We make interrogative sentences with there was and there were by putting was/were at the beginning of the sentence.

We give an affirmative short answer with there was/there:
Yes, + there + was/were.
Yes, there was.
Yes, there were.
We give an negative short answer with there was/were:
No, + there + wasn't/weren't.
No, there wasn't.
No, there weren't.

Fill in the blank with the correct month

1. January, February, _____.

2. _____, November, December

3. May, _____, July.

4. _____, September, October.

5. April, _____, June.

Choose the sentence that is correct

1. Which is correct?
   ☐ There were a festival last month.
   ☐ There was a festival last month.
2. Which is correct?
   ☐ Was there a party yesterday?
   ☐ There was a party yesterday?
3. Which is correct?
   ☐ Were there many festivities last year?
   ☐ There were many festivities last year?
4. Which is correct?
   ☐ No there wasn't
   ☐ No, there wasn't.
5. Which is correct?
   ☐ Yes, there was.
   ☐ Yes there was

How well did you do in this unit?

Write the CAN DO statement and assess yourself.

Write 3, 2, or 1

3 = VERY WELL
2 = WELL
1 = NOT SO WELL

I CAN...
_____
_____
_____
_____
_____
_____
_____

Level FIVE Unit ELEVEN
Let's learn about hobbies!

11.1
Vocabulary

Learn the hobbies

play video games

paint

play guitar

yoga

knit

watch tv

sew

bake

11.2 Dialogs

Level FIVE Unit ELEVEN
Let's learn about hobbies!

Practice the dialogs

What is your hobby?
- I play video games all the time.
Really?
-Really! In fact, I was playing video games a moment ago.
Great!

What is your hobby?
-We knit all the time.
Really?
-Really! In fact, we were knitting a moment ago.
Great!

What is Lucy's hobby?
-She paints all the time.
Really?
-Really! In fact, she was painting a moment ago.
Great!

What is Andy and Tony's hobby?
-They bake all the time.
Really?
-Really! In fact, they were baking a moment ago.
Great!

What is Tony's hobby?
 -He watches TV all the time.
Really?
-Really! In fact, he was watching TV a moment ago.
Great!

What is _____ hobby?
- He _____ all the time.
Really?
-Really! In fact, he was _____ a moment ago.
Great!

Now you!

Level FIVE Unit ELEVEN
Let's learn about hobbies!

11.3 Vocabulary

Our hobbies

Yesterday in class, our teacher Miss Patty was telling us all about hobbies that they are fun and entertaining.
Now I know what hobbies my friends have. How do I know? Well, I called them yesterday after school and asked them.
Sandy was playing video games, she plays them all the time. And she also loves to knit.
She says they are the best hobbies ever!
Andy was playing the guitar; he plays it all the time too; and he also likes to bake.
Lucy was painting, she loves to paint and just like Sandy, she likes to knit too.
Tony was watching TV; he watches all the time. And like Andy, he likes to bake also; their cookies are delicious.
My friends have great hobbies! What is my hobby? I love yoga!
What is your hobby?

Match the beginning of the sentence with the image that completes the idea

Sandy was (__)
Andy was (__)
Lucy was (__)
Tony was (__)
I love (__)

a)  b)   c)

d)   e)

Read the text and circle true or false

1. Andy was baking.
    true   false
2. Tony was watching TV.
    true   false
3. Lucy was knitting.
    true   false
4. Sandy was playing video games.
    true   false
5. Sandy loves to bake.
    true   false
6. Tony likes to play the guitar.
    true   false

11.4 Writing

Level FIVE Unit ELEVEN
Let's learn about hobbies!

Choose the verb+ing and a hobby and fill the blanks. Be careful to choose from the correct box. You can use several times each word. Then read aloud.

Our hobbies

Yesterday in class, our teacher Miss Patty was telling us all about hobbies that they are fun and entertaining.
Now I know what hobbies my friends have. How do I know? Well, I called them yesterday after school and asked them.
Sandy was (1)_____ . And she also loves to (2)_____.
She says they are the best hobbies ever!
Andy was (1)_____; and he also likes to (2)_____.
Lucy was (1)_____, she loves to (2)_____ and just like Sandy, she likes to (2)_____ too.
Tony was (1)_____. And like Andy, he likes to (2)_____ also.
My friends have great hobbies! What is my hobby? I love yoga!
Waht is your hobby? I love to (2)_____.

1) knitting / sewing / doing yoga / baking / playing guitar / watching TV / painting / playing video games

2) to knit / to sew / to do yoga / to bake / to play guitar / to watch TV / to paint / to play video games

Level FIVE Unit ELEVEN
Let's learn about hobbies!

11.5 Language in use

The Past Progressive Tense is used to describe an action that was in progress at a specific time in the past.

Affirmative:
Subjet + BE past + verb_ING + complement

I was playing video games after school yesterday.
She was watching TV.
They were baking cookies.

Unscramble the sentences

1. _____ _____ _____ _____.
watching / was / I / TV

2. _____ _____ _____ _____ _____.
Andy / the / guitar / playing was

3. _____ _____ _____ _____ _____.
Sandy / video / games playing / was

4. _____ _____ _____ _____ _____ _____.
Tony / Andy / cookies baking / were / and

5. _____ _____ _____ _____ _____.
Lucy / knitting / and / were Sandy

Find the words below

W	B	A	K	E	V	H	G	B	G	T
V	F	E	Y	N	I	K	M	P	E	A
F	T	Z	N	S	D	F	E	R	E	D
R	N	H	T	Z	E	C	W	D	S	F
S	A	I	C	D	O	Y	S	Y	Z	Z
Y	N	C	L	T	G	Q	T	B	J	M
K	O	D	O	V	A	K	N	U	Q	R
W	N	G	J	E	M	W	I	S	M	R
J	C	F	A	F	E	N	A	E	K	M
D	X	F	F	S	S	G	P	W	B	D
T	N	E	M	R	R	T	S	N	I	R

VIDEO GAMES   KNIT
PAINT   SEW
INSTRUMENT   BAKE
WATCH TV   YOGA

73

How well did you do in this unit?
Write the CAN DO statement and assess yourself.
Write 3, 2, or 1
3 = VERY WELL
2 = WELL
1 = NOT SO WELL

I CAN...

_____
_____
_____
_____
_____
_____

Level FIVE Unit TWELVE
Let's learn about leisure activities!

12.1
Vocabulary

Learn the leisure activities

camping

cycling

karate

surfing the internet

surfing

skating

running

playing computer games

12.2 Dialogs

Level FIVE Unit TWELVE
Let's learn about leisure activities!

Practice the dialogs

Was Sandy busy yesterday?
-Not really. She wasn't running as usual.
Why not?
-I don't know.

Was Tony busy yesterday?
-Not really. He wasn't cycling as usual.
Why not?
-I don't know.

Was Andy busy yesterday?
-Not really. He wasn't surfing the internet as usual.
Why not?
-I don't know.

Was Tom busy yesterday?
-Not really. He wasn't surfing as usual.
Why not?
-I don't know.

Were Harry and Lucy busy yesterday?
-Not really. They weren't practicing karate as usual.
Why not?
-I don't know.

Were Andy and Sandy busy yesterday?
-Not really. They weren't playing games as usual.
Why not?
-I don't know.

Were/was _____ busy yesterday?
-Not really _____ weren't/wasn't _____ as usual..
Why not?
-I don't know.

Now you!

Level FIVE Unit TWELVE
Let's learn about leisure activities!

12.3 Reading

Not as usual

Yesterday was a very strange afternoon. What my students usually do after school, they weren't doing yesterday. Let me explain…

Andy and Sandy usually play computer games after school; but they weren't playing computer games yesterday. Harry and Lucy usually practice karate but they weren't practicing karate yesterday. Tom wasn't surfing as usual; and that is strange because he loves to surf. Andy wasn't surfing the internet as usual; and he never misses a day of surfing the internet in the afternoon. Tony wasn't cycling as usual; he loves to cycle in the park. And Sandy wasn't running as usual; that is really strange, she cannot live one day without running.

What were my students doing after school then? They weren't doing their usual after-school activities.

I certainly don't know. I will have to ask them tomorrow!

Complete the sentences with the correct name

Tony / Sandy / Lucy / Andy / Harry / Tom

1. _____ wasn't running as usual.

2. _____ wasn't cycling.

3. _____ wasn't surfing the internet.

4. _____ wasn't practicing karate.

5. _____ wasn't playing computer games.

Circle ✓ if the sentence is correct
Circle ✗ if the sentence is wrong

1. Sandy wasn't playing computer games. ✗ ✓

2. Lucy wasn't surfing yesterday. ✗ ✓

3. Harry wasn't practicing karate as usual. ✗ ✓

4. Tom wasn't surfing the internet. ✗ ✓

5. Sandy wasn't cycling as usual. ✗ ✓

12.4 Writing

Level FIVE Unit TWELVE
Let's learn about leisure activities!

Choose any leisure activity and fill the blanks. You can use several times each word. Then read aloud.

Not as usual

Yesterday was a very strange afternoon. What my students usually do after school, they weren't doing yesterday. Let me explain…
Andy and Sandy usually _____ after school; but they weren't _____ yesterday. Harry and Lucy usually _____ but they weren't _____ yesterday. Tom wasn't _____ as usual; and that is strange because he loves to _____.
Andy wasn't _____ as usual; and he never misses day of _____ in the afternoon. Tony wasn't _____ as usual; he loves to _____ in the park. And Sandy wasn't _____ as usual; that is really strange, she cannot live one day without _____.
What were my students doing after school then? They weren't doing their usual after-school activities. I certainly don't know. I will have to ask them tomorrow!

camping/ cycling/ practicing/ running/ skating/ surfing/ surfing internet/ playing computer games

Level FIVE Unit TWELVE
Let's learn about leisure activities!

12.5 Language in use

The Past Progressive Tense is used to describe an action that was in progress at a specific time in the past.

Negative:
Subject + BE past + NOT + verb-ING + complement

I wasn't surfing the internet after school yesterday.
She wasn't running.
They weren't practicing karate.

Choose the sentence that is correct

1. Which is correct?
   ☐ Sandy wasn't skating.
   ☐ Sandy weren't skating.
2. Which is correct?
   ☐ I weren't surfing the internet.
   ☐ I wasn't surfing the internet.
3. Which is correct?
   ☐ We weren't running in the park.
   ☐ We wasn't running in the park.
4. Which is correct?
   ☐ They wasn't camping.
   ☐ They weren't camping.
5. Which is correct?
   ☐ Tony wasn't practicing karate.
   ☐ Tony weren't practicing karate.

Tongue Twister Time.

While we were walking
We were watching
Window washers
Wash Washington's Windows
With warm water.

How well did you do in this unit?
Write the CAN DO statement and assess yourself.
Write 3, 2, or 1
3 = VERY WELL
2 = WELL
1 = NOT SO WELL

I CAN...
_____
_____
_____
_____
_____
_____

Level FIVE Unit THIRTEEN
Let's learn about hobbies at home!

13.1
Vocabulary

Learn the hobbies

13.2 Dialogs

Level FIVE Unit THIRTEEN
Let's learn about hobbies at home!

Practice the dialogs

Were you playing guitar yesterday?
-Yes, I was. I was playing guitar in the yard.

Was Sandy writing yesterday?
-Yes, she was. She was writing in her bedroom.

Was Lucy sewing a dress yesterday?
-Yes, she was. She was sewing in the dining room.

Were you and Harry baking cookies yesterday?
-Yes, we were. We were baking in the kitchen.

Were Tony and Lucy doing yoga yesterday?
-Yes, they were.
  They were doing yoga in the basement.

Was ___ _____ yesterday?
-Yes, ___ ____. _____.

Now you!

Level FIVE Unit THIRTEEN
Let's learn about hobbies at home!

13.3 Reading

Relaxing at Home

It is so relaxing to enjoy your hobbies at home. My hobby is to play the guitar; I usually play the guitar inside the house but yesterday was a great day, the weather was warm so I was playing the guitar in the yard all afternoon.

Lucy has a hobby too. She likes to write, she writes poems, she writes in her diary, she writes everything she thinks about; she was writing in her bedroom all afternoon.

Sandy's hobby is sewing; she sews dresses for her dolls. She was sewing in the dining room; her mom helps her a lot.

Tony and Harry were baking cookies together in the kitchen. Their cookies are always delicious.

Harry was at Lucy's house they were doing yoga in the basement.

Tom has a cool hobby! He likes to play video games. He was playing in his special place: the attic!

Yes, yesterday was a great day to enjoy hobbies.
Do you have a hobby?

Complete the sentences according to the reading

attic / basement / bathroom
bedroom / dining room/ kitchen
living room / yard

1. Andy was playing guitar in the _____.

2. Tony and Harry were baking cookies in the _____.

3. Lucy was writing in the _____.

4. Harry and Lucy were doing yoga in the _____.

5. Sandy was sewing in the _____.

Based on the reading choose true or false

1. Andy was playing the guitar in the living room.
   true   false

2. Tom was playing video games in the attic.
   true   false

3. Sandy was sewing in the dining room.
   true   false

4. Tony and Harry were baking cookies in the yard.
   true   false

5. Harry and Lucy were doing yoga in the basement.
   true   false

13.4 Writing

Level FIVE Unit THIRTEEN
Let's learn about hobbies at home!

Choose a room in the house and fill the blanks. You can use several times each word. Then read aloud.

Relaxing at home

It is so relaxing to enjoy your hobbies at home.
My hobby is to play the guitar;
I was playing the guitar in the _____ all afternoon.
Lucy has a hobby too. She likes to write,
she writes poems, she writes in her diary, she writes everything
she thinks about; she was writing in her _____ all afternoon.
Sandy's hobby is sewing; she sews dresses for her dolls.
She was sewing in the _____; her mom helps her a lot.
Tony and Harry were baking cookies together in the _____.
Their cookies are always delicious.
Harry was at Lucy's house they were doing yoga in the _____.
Tom has a cool hobby! He likes to play video games.
He was playing in his special place: the _____!
Yes, yesterday was a great day to enjoy hobbies.
Do you have a hobby?
Where do you enjoy your hobby? _____

attic / basement / bathroom / bedroom / dining room
kitchen / living room / yard

Level FIVE Unit THIRTEEN
Let's learn about hobbies at home!

13.5 Language in use

The Past Progressive Tense is used to describe an action that was in progress at a specific time in the past.

Interrogative
BE past + subject + verb_ING + complement
Was Sandy sewing in the dining room?

Short affirmative answer
Yes, (comma) personal pronoun + BE past. (period)
Yes, she was.

Choose the correct short affirmative answer

1. Was Sandy sewing in the dining room?
   ☐ Yes, she was. ☐ Yes, he was.
   ☐ Yes, Sandy was.
2. Was Tom playing video games in the attic?
   ☐ Yes, Tom was. ☐ Yes, he was.
   ☐ Yes, she was.
3. Were Harry and Lucy doing yoga in the basement?
   ☐ Yes, Harry and Lucy were.
   ☐ Yes, they were.
   ☐ Yes, you were.
4. Were you and Harry baking cookies in the kitchen?
   ☐ Yes, I was. ☐ Yes, you were.
   ☐ Yes, we were

Complete the short affirmative answers

1. Was Sandy sewing in the dining room?
   - Yes, _____ _____.
2. Were you playing the guitar in the yard?
   - Yes, _____ _____.
3. Were you and Harry baking cookies in the kitchen?
   - Yes, _____ _____.
4. Were Harry and Lucy doing yoga in the basement?
   - Yes, _____ _____.
5. Was Tom playing video games in the attic?
   - Yes, _____ _____.

How well did you do in this unit?

Write the CAN DO statement and assess yourself.

Write 3, 2, or 1

3 = VERY WELL

2 = WELL

1 = NOT SO WELL

I CAN...

_____

_____

_____

_____

_____

_____

Level FIVE Unit FOURTEEN
Let's learn about sports!

14.1 Vocabulary

Learn the sports

badminton

skateboarding

baseball

golf

bowling

tennis

basketball

volleyball

football

soccer

14.2 Dialogs

Level FIVE Unit FOURTEEN
Let's learn about sports!

Practice the dialogs

Were you playing badminton yesterday?
-No, I wasn't. I was skateboarding.

Was Tony playing football yesterday?
-No, he wasn't. He was playing soccer.

Was Lucy bowling yesterday?
-No, she wasn't. She was playing tennis.

Were you and Lucy playing basketball?
-No, we weren't. We were playing volleyball.

Were Harry and Andy playing baseball?
-No, they weren't. They were playing golf.

Was/Were _____ _____ ?
-No, _____ _____. _____.

Now you!

Level FIVE Unit FOURTEEN
Let's learn about sports!

14.3
Reading

Sports, sports, sports!

I love sports; I want to play sports every day, in the morning, in the afternoon, at night! My mother says that I have to study first, but I like to play sports more.
Yesterday was Saturday and I wasn't playing basketball in the morning I was playing volleyball and I was so happy playing.
My friends like sports too. I called them to see what they were playing.
Andy was skateboarding, he wasn't playing badminton; he says playing badminton is for Sunday afternoons.
My friend Tony wasn't playing soccer.
He plays soccer on Sunday morning.
Lucy was playing tennis; she wasn't bowling.
And Harry was playing baseball; he wasn't playing golf.
He plays golf on Sundays with his dad.
Certainly my friends and I love sports!
Do you like sports? What sports do you like?

Read carefully. Give short answers.

1. Was Sandy playing basketball?
   ____ , ____ ____ .

2. Was Andy skateboarding?
   ____ , ____ ____ .

3. Was Tony playing soccer?
   ____ , ____ ____ .

4. Was Lucy bowling?
   ____ , ____ ____ .

5. Was Harry playing baseball?
   ____ , ____ ____ .

Choose the right answer

1. Was Andy playing badminton?
   ☐ Yes, he was.   ☐ No, he wasn't.

2. Was Lucy playing tennis?
   ☐ Yes, she was.   ☐ No, she wasn't

3. Was Tony playing soccer?
   ☐ Yes, he was.   ☐ No, he wasn't

4. Was Harry playing golf?
   ☐ Yes, he was.   ☐ No, he wasn't.

5. Was Sandy playing volleyball?
   ☐ Yes, she was.   ☐ No, she wasn't

14.4 Writing

Level FIVE Unit FOURTEEN
Let's learn about sports!

Choose a sport and fill the blanks. You can use several times each word. Then read aloud.

Sports, Sports, Sports!

I love sports; I want to play sports every day, in the morning, in the afternoon, at night! My mother says that I have to study first, but I like to play sports more.

Yesterday was Saturday and I wasn't playing _____ in the morning I was playing _____ and I was so happy playing. My friends like sports too. I called them to see what they were playing.

Andy was _____, he wasn't playing _____;
he says playing _____ is for Sunday afternoons.
My friend Tony wasn't playing _____.
He plays _____ on Sunday morning.
Lucy was _____ tennis; she wasn't _____.
And Harry was playing _____; he wasn't playing _____.
He plays _____ on Sundays with his dad.
Certainly my friends and I love sports!
Do you like sports? What sports do you like? I like _____.

badminton • baseball • basketball • bowling
football • golf • skateboarding • soccer • tennis • volleyball

Level FIVE Unit FOURTEEN
Let's learn about sports!

14.5 Language in use

The Past Progressive Tense is used to describe an action that was in progress at a specific time in the past.

Interrogative
BE past + subject + verb-ING + complement
Was Sandy sewing in the dining room?

Short negative answer
No, (comma) personal pronoun + BE past-NOT. (period)
No, she wasn't.

Choose the correct short negative answer

1. Was Andy playing baseball?
   - No, Andy wasn't.
   - No, he wasn't.
   - No he wasn't

2. Were Harry And Tony playing soccer?
   - No, Harry and Tony weren't.
   - No they weren't
   - No, they weren't.

3. Was Lucy playing golf?
   - No, she wasn't.
   - No, Lucy wasn't.
   - No she wasn't

4. Were you and Sandy playing baseball?
   - No we weren't
   - No, we weren't.
   - No Sandy and me weren't.

Complete the short negative answers

1. Was Andy playing badminton?
   - No, _____ _____.

2. Was Lucy playing tennis?
   - No, _____ _____.

3. Were Tony and Harry playing soccer?
   - No, _____ _____.

4. Were you and Harry playing golf?
   - No, _____ _____.

5. Were you playing volleyball?
   - No, _____ _____.

How well did you do in this unit?

Write the CAN DO statement and assess yourself.
Write 3, 2, or 1
3 = VERY WELL
2 = WELL
1 = NOT SO WELL

I CAN...

_____
_____
_____
_____
_____
_____
_____

Level FIVE Unit FIFTEEN
Let's learn about more hobbies!

15.1
Vocabulary

Learn the hobbies

park

cycling

rink

skating

beach

jogging

home

playing

park

running

Unscramble the words

1. __ __ __ __ __ __ __
   c / c / l / n / g / i / y
2. __ __ __ __ __ __ __
   u / i / g / n / n / n / r
3. __ __ __ __ __ __ __
   j / g / o / n / g / i / g
4. __ __ __ __ __ __ __
   y / p / g / l / n / a / i
5. __ __ __ __ __ __ __
   t / a / k / s / g / n / i

15.2 Dialogs

Level FIVE Unit FIFTEEN
Let's learn about more hobbies!

Practice the dialogs

What were you doing yesterday?
-I was cycling.
Cycling? Where were you cycling?
-I was cycling in the park.
Cool!

What was Andy doing yesterday?
-He was playing video games.
Video games? Where was he playing video games?
-He was playing in his home.
Cool!

What was Sandy doing yesterday?
-She was running.
Running? Where was she running?
-She was running in the park.
Cool!

What was Harry doing yesterday?
-He was skating.
Skating? Where was he skating?
-He was skating in the rink.
Cool!

What was _____ doing yesterday?
-He/She was _____.
_____? Where was he/she _____?
-He/She was _____ _____
Cool!

Now you!

Level FIVE Unit FIFTEEN
Let's learn about more hobbies!

15.3 Reading

What were you doing?

My friends and I were having so much fun yesterday.
We were all doing the things that we enjoy the most.
My friend Sandy was running in the park; there are races
every weekend. She runs very fast, she loves to run.
Lucy was jogging at the beach;
she likes the fresh air when she jogs.
Andy was playing video games at home with his cousins.
He says he usually wins; he is pretty good.
Harry was skating in the skating rink. The skating rink is so cool,
they skate 'round and 'round while great music is playing.
Harry says that is why he likes to skate so much.
And what was I doing? Well my favorite thing is cycling.
And yesterday I was cycling in the park;
there is a special place to cycle in this park,
I go there every chance I have.
What were you doing yesterday?

Answer the questions

1. Where were you cycling?
   _____.
2. Where was Sandy running?
   _____.
3. Where was Andy playing video games?
   _____.
4. Where was Harry skating?
   _____.
5. Where was Lucy jogging?
   _____.

Choose the right answer

1. Who was skating?
   ☐ Sandy   ☐ Andy   ☐ Harry
2. Who was running?
   ☐ Sandy   ☐ Andy   ☐ Harry
3. Who was playing video games?
   ☐ Andy   ☐ Tony   ☐ Lucy
4. Who was cycling?
   ☐ Andy   ☐ Tony   ☐ Lucy
5. Who was jogging?
   ☐ Andy   ☐ Tony   ☐ Lucy

15.4 Writing

Level FIVE Unit FIFTEEN
Let's learn about more hobbies!

Choose a hobby and a place then fill the blanks. You can use several times each word. Be careful to choose from the correct box. Then read aloud.

What were you doing?

My friends and I were having so much fun yesterday.
We were all doing the things that we enjoy the most.
My friend Sandy was (1) _____ (2) _____.
Lucy was (1) _____ (2) _____.
Andy was (1) _____ (2) _____.
Harry was (1) _____ (2) _____.
And what was I doing? Well my favorite thing is (1) _____ (2) _____.
What were you doing yesterday?

1) running • jogging • cycling • skating • playing video games

2) In the park • at the beach • in the park • in the rink • at home

Level FIVE Unit FIFTEEN
Let's learn about more hobbies!

15.5 Language in use

The Past Progressive Tense is used to describe an action that was in progress at a specific time in the past.

WH-questions
Wh + BE-past + subject + verb-ING + complement?

What was Sandy doing yesterday?

Where was Sandy running?

Choose and write the correct answer

> At 8:00 o'clock / In the park
> Running / Sandy / Yesterday

1. What were you doing?
   _____.

2. Where were you cycling?
   _____.

3. When were you skating?
   _____.

4. Who was running in the park?
   _____.

5. What time were you jogging?
   _____.

Unscramble the sentences

1. _____ _____ _____ _____ _____
   doing / were / what / you / ?

2. _____ _____ _____ _____ _____
   ? / playing / Sandy / what / was

3. _____ _____ _____ _____ _____
   Andy / ? / running / where / was

4. _____ _____ _____ _____ _____
   Lucy / ? / was / jogging / Where

5. _____ _____ _____ _____ _____
   ? / they / were / where / cycling

97

How well did you do in this unit?
Write the CAN DO statement and assess yourself.
Write 3, 2, or 1
3 = VERY WELL
2 = WELL
1 = NOT SO WELL

I CAN...
_____
_____
_____
_____
_____
_____

Level SIX Unit ONE
Let's learn about verbs!

16.1
Vocabulary

Learn the verbs

brush

brushed

fix

fixed

kick

kicked

like

liked

ask

asked

look

looked

walk

walked

search

searched

work

worked

talk

talked

16.2 Dialogs

Practice the dialogs

I asked the teacher many questions yesterday.
-Really, why?
Because she has all the answers.

Sandy brushed her hair 100 times yesterday.
-Really, why?
Because she likes shiny hair.

Sandy and I kicked the soccer ball 50 times yesterday.
-Really, why?
Because we want to be good soccer players.

Tony fixed his bike yesterday.
-Really, why?
Because his bike was broken.

Sandy and Lucy talked all afternoon yesterday.
-Really, why?
Because they are good friends.

_____ _____ all afternoon yesterday.
-Really, why?
Because _____.

Level SIX Unit ONE
Let's learn about verbs!

16.3 Reading

Yesterday

Sandy and I talked and talked for a long time yesterday, we are good friends and there is always something new to talk about. We talked about so many things; like that yesterday. Andy asked our teacher a lot of questions; Andy says that our teacher always has all the answers. Then we talked about Tony; that he fixed his bike yesterday, he is very good at fixing things. Then we talked about her hair, that it was shiny, and it is because she brushed it 100 times! We also talked about how Sandy and Harry train to become good soccer players. They kicked the ball more than 50 times without stopping! We also talked about how Andy and Harry worked so hard this week at school. After we talked Sandy and I were thirsty so we walked to the corner store to buy some water. I liked my afternoon with my best friend Sandy. I hope we have many more afternoons like yesterday. Who is your best friend? Do you talk about everything?

Complete the sentences

(4x)
Andy / Tony / Harry / Lucy / Sandy

1. _____ and _____ talked for a long time.
2. _____ asked many questions.
3. _____ fixed his bike.
4. _____ brushed her hair.
5. _____ and _____ kicked the soccer ball.
6. _____ and _____ worked at school.
7. _____ and _____ walked to the corner store.

Choose true or false

1. Sandy and Lucy talked for a short time yesterday. ✓ ✗
2. Andy asked the teacher a lot of questions. ✓ ✗
3. Tony fixed his computer yesterday. ✓ ✗
4. Sandy brushed her hair 10 times. ✓ ✗
5. Sandy and Harry kicked the soccer ball. ✓ ✗
6. We walked to the school. ✓ ✗

101

16.4 Writing

Level SIX Unit ONE
Let's learn about verbs!

Choose a verb and fill the blanks. You can use several times each word. Then read aloud.

Yesterday

Sandy and I talked for a long time yesterday, we are good friends and there is always something new to talk about. Yesterday we talked about what our friends did all day:

Andy _____.
Tony _____.
Sandy _____.
Sandy and Harry _____.
Andy and Harry _____.
Then, Sandy and I _____.
And finally I _____.

I hope we have many more afternoons like yesterday.
Who is your best friend? Do you talk about everything?

---

asked questions • brushed his/her hair • fixed the bike
kicked the ball • liked the afternoon • talked to my friend
walked to the store • worked at school

Level SIX Unit ONE
Let's learn about verbs!

16.5 Language in use

Simple Past Tense of Regular Verbs

We use the simple past tense to describe an action that occurred and was completed in the past.
The simple past is formed by adding -ed to the base form of the verb.
If the infinitive of the verb has a voiceless sound at the end of it, such as: p, k, s, ch, sh, f, x, h: we pronounce the "ed" as a "T"

- ask - asked
- brush - brushed
- fix - fixed
- kick - kicked
- like - liked
- look - looked
- match - matched
- search - searched
- talk - talked
- walk - walked
- work - worked

Tongue Twister Time

Peter Piper picked a peck of pickled peppers.
A peck of pickled peppers Peter Piper picked.
If Peter Piper picked a peck of pickled peppers,
Where's the peck of pickled peppers Peter Piper picked?

Label the verbs in present and past

How well did you do in this unit?
Write the CAN DO statement and assess yourself.
Write 3, 2, or 1
3 = VERY WELL
2 = WELL
1 = NOT SO WELL

I CAN...

_____
_____
_____
_____
_____
_____

Level SIX Unit TWO
Let's learn about action words!

17.1
Vocabulary

Learn the action words

improve / improved

save / saved

receive / received

travel / traveled

explain / explained

burn / burned

observe / observed

turn / turned

pull / pulled

105

17.2 Dialogs

Level SIX Unit TWO
Let's learn about action words!

Practice the dialogs

Miss Patty explained the lesson, right?
-Yes, she explained the lesson twice… why?
Just asking!

Tony burned his fingers, right?
-Yes, he burned two fingers… why?
Just asking!

You received some e-mails, right?
-Yes, I received ten e-mails yesterday… why?
Just asking!

Lucy and her sister saved some money, right?
-Yes, they saved 100 dollars… why?
Just asking!

You and Harry observed the experiment, right?
-Yes, we observed it for an hour… why?
Just asking!

_____ _____, right?
-Yes, _____… why?
Just asking!

Now you!

Level SIX Unit TWO
Let's learn about action words!

17.3 Reading

Just asking!

Miss Patty asked me to talk to friends and get information from them about different things. She said that I will win a prize, if I can get a lot of information in 5 minutes! So I started immediately!
This is the information I collected:
Tony burned two of his fingers.
Andy received ten e-mails yesterday. Harry traveled in the summer.
Lucy and her sister saved 100 dollars. Tony and Harry observed the experiment for an hour. Andy improved his grades by two points. Tom turned off the lights in the classroom.
Finally, Miss Patty explained the lesson about the past tense twice; this information was part of the lesson.
And what is my prize?
A shiny star sticker for my collection. Thanks Miss Patty!

Match both parts of the sentences

1. Andy improved (___)
2. Miss Patty explained (___)
3. Tony burned (___)
4. Andy received (___)
5. Harry traveled (___)

a) in the summer.
b) ten e-mails.
c) two of his fingers.
d) the lesson twice.
e) his grades.

Read and circle true or false according to the reading

1. Miss Patty explained the lesson three times.
   true   false

2. Tony burned two of his fingers.
   true   false

3. Andy received one e-mail.
   true   false

4. Tom traveled last summer.
   true   false

5. Sandy improved her grades.
   true   false

17.4 Writing

Level SIX Unit TWO
Let's learn about action words!

Choose a verb-phrase and fill the blanks. You can use several times each word. Then read aloud.

Just asking!

Miss Patty asked me to talk to friends and get information from them about different things. She said that I will win a prize, if I can get a lot of information in 5 minutes! So I started immediately!
This is the information I collected:

Tony _____.
Andy _____ yesterday.
Harry _____.
Lucy and her sister _____.
Tony and Harry _____.
Andy _____.
Tom _____.
Finally, Miss Patty _____.

And what is my prize?
A shiny star sticker for my collection. Thanks Miss Patty!

---

arrived 15 minutes late • burned two fingers
explained the lesson twice • improved grades
observed the experiment • pulled the door • received 10 e-mails
saved a hundred dollars • traveled in the summer
turned off the lights

Level SIX Unit TWO
Let's learn about action words!

17.5 Language in use

Simple Past Tense of Regular Verbs

We use the simple past tense to describe an action that occurred and was completed in the past. The simple past is formed by adding -ed to the base form of the verb. If the verb already ends in an "e" just add "d". If the last letter of the words ends in a voiced consonant, then the "ED" is pronounced like a "D"

down

1. Andy _____ his grades.
2. Lucy and her sister _____ $100 dlls.
4. Andy _____ ten e-mails.
6. Tony _____ two of his fingers.

across

3. Harry _____ in the summer.
5. Tony and Harry _____ the experiment.
7. I _____ off the lights.
8. Miss Patty _____ the lesson twice.

How well did you do in this unit?

Write the CAN DO statement and assess yourself.

Write 3, 2, or 1

3 = VERY WELL

2 = WELL

1 = NOT SO WELL

I CAN...

_____

_____

_____

_____

_____

_____

Level SIX Unit THREE
Let's learn about plants and flowers!

18.1
Vocabulary

Learn the plants and flowers

accept

accepted

decide

decided

need

needed

start

started

wait

waited

plant

planted

bush

carnations

roses

daisies

pines

18.2 Dialogs

Level SIX Unit THREE
Let's learn about plants and flowers!

Practice the dialogs

I planted some pines in my yard last April.
-Really, why?
Because it was Earth Day.
-Oh, I see!

Sandy accepted some roses from Andy last week.
-Really, why?
Because it was Sandy's birthday.
-Oh, I see!

My dad and my brother decided to buy daisies for my mom.
-Really, why?
Because it was Mother's Day.
-Oh, I see!

Harry and I waited behind the bushes after school yesterday.
-Really, why?
Because it was Surprise a Friend Day.
-Oh, I see!

Lucy needed some carnations last Monday.
-Really, why?
Because it was Science Fair Day.
-Oh, I see!

_____ needed _____ last Monday.
-Really, why?
Because it was _____.
-Oh, I see!

Now you!

Level SIX Unit THREE
Let's learn about plants and flowers!

18.3 Reading

Plants and flowers

Miss Patty was telling us about the importance of plants and flowers in class this week. She says that plants apart from being beautiful help the environment. So our class decided to plant flowers, plants, trees and bushes in our homes and at school. I planted some pine trees in my back yard. Andy decided to plant some daisies and roses too. Harry waited for the bushes in his garden to grow a little bit more to cut them in some nice shape. We also had Science Fair and Lucy needed some carnations to show us how they change color, it was amazing! After all we talked about in class this week, Tom started to plant flowers in his garden too! Yes, plants, trees and flowers are beautiful and are necessary for a good environment. Do you like plants? What flowers do you like?

According to the reading circle the correct answer

1. Who planted pine trees?
   Tom   Sandy   Andy

2. Who decided to plant daisies?
   Tom   Sandy   Andy

3. Who waited for the bushes to grow?
   Harry   Andy   Tony

4. Who needed carnations for Science Fair?
   Sandy   Lucy   Tony

5. Who started to plant flowers in his garden?
   Tom   Lucy   Harry

Read and answer true or false according to the reading

1. Plants are good for the environment.
   true   false

2. I planted flowers in my back yard.
   true   false

3. Andy decided to plant daisies.
   true   false

4. Harry waited for the bushes to grow.
   true   false

5. Lucy needed roses for Science Fair.
   true   false

6. Tom started to plant flowers.
   true   false

18.4 Writing

Level SIX Unit THREE
Let's learn about plants and flowers!

Choose a verb-phrase and fill the blanks. You can use several times each word. Then read aloud.

Plants and flowers

Miss Patty was telling us about the importance of plants and flowers in class this week. She says that plants apart from being beautiful help the environment.
So our class decided to plant flowers, plants, trees and bushes in our homes and at school.
Sandy _____ in her yard last April, because it was Earth Day.
Lucy _____ from Andy last week. Because it was her birthday.
My dad and my brother _____ for my mom.
Because it was Mother's Day.
Harry and I _____ after school yesterday.
Because it was Surprise a Friend Day.
Lucy _____ last Monday. Because it was Science Fair Day.
Tom _____ last Sunday. Because it was Spring Day.

---

accepted some flowers • decided to buy daisies
needed some carnations • planted some pines
started to plant roses • waited behind the bushes

Level SIX Unit THREE
Let's learn about plants and flowers!

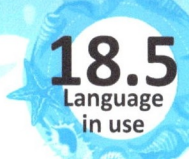

Simple Past Tense of Regular Verbs

We use the simple past tense to describe an action that occurred and was completed in the past. The simple past is formed by adding –ed to the base form of the verb.
If the last letter of the words ends in "d" or "t", then the "ed" is pronounced as a complete syllable.
need - needed

Complete the sentences with the correct form of the verbs from the box

accept / decide / need
plant / start / wait

1. I _____ some pines in my yard last April.

2. Sandy _____ some roses from Andy last week.

3. My dad and my brother _____ to buy daisies for my mom.

4. Harry and I _____ behind the bushes after school yesterday.

5. Lucy _____ some carnations last Monday.

6. Tom _____ to plant flowers last Sunday.

Unscramble the verbs

1. __ __ __ __ __ __ __ __
   d / e / t / p / a / c / c / e

2. __ __ __ __ __ __ __
   d / e / d / d / e / c / i

3. __ __ __ __ __ __
   d / d / e / e / e / n

4. __ __ __ __ __ __ __
   t / e / d / n / a / l / p

5. __ __ __ __ __ __ __
   s / t / r / t / d / a / e

6. __ __ __ __ __ __
   a / i / e / w / t / d

How well did you do in this unit?
Write the CAN DO statement and assess yourself.
Write 3, 2, or 1
3 = VERY WELL
2 = WELL
1 = NOT SO WELL

I CAN...
_____
_____
_____
_____
_____
_____
_____

Level SIX Unit FOUR
Let's learn about school activities!

Learn the school activities

ask / asked

color / colored

explain / explained

search / searched

talk / talked

work / worked

start / started

end / ended

walk / walked

19.2 Dialogs

Level SIX Unit FOUR
Let's learn about school activities!

Practice the dialogs

Did Andy search for the new words yesterday?
-Yes, he searched for the new words.

Did you and Sandy talk during recess yesterday?
-Yes, we talked during recess.

Did Miss Patty explain the past tense yesterday?
-Yes, she explained the past tense.

Did Harry and Lucy walk home from school yesterday?
-Yes, they walked home from school.

Did you ask a lot of questions yesterday?
-Yes, I asked a lot of questions.

Did _____ yesterday?
-Yes, _____.

Yesterday

It was a long day at school yesterday.
We were very busy during all the classes.
I asked so many questions that Miss Patty explained
all about the Past Tense during our English class again and again.
Andy searched for 20 new verbs in the dictionary during class.
Lucy colored the pictures in her notebook, she colors so pretty.
Tom and Lucy even worked during recess. Sandy and I just talked;
we talked about the homework and other things.
The class finally ended at 12 o'clock;
so we started to pick up our things to go home.
Harry and Lucy walked home.
They were so tired. It certainly was a long day at school yesterday.
How was your day at school yesterday? Did you work very hard?

According to the reading complete the sentences with the corresponding name

Andy / Harry and Lucy / Lucy / Miss Patty / Sandy and Tony / Tom and Lucy / Tony

1. _____ asked a lot of questions
2. _____ explained the past tense.
3. _____ searched for new verbs.
4. _____ colored pictures.
5- _____ worked over recess.
6- _____ talked during recess.
7- _____ walked home.

Answer the questions with complete sentences

1. Did Tony ask a lot of questions?
   Yes, _____.

2. Did Miss Patty explain about the past tense?
   Yes, _____.

3. Did Andy search for 20 verbs in the dictionary?
   Yes, _____.

4. Did Lucy color pictures in her notebook?
   Yes, _____.

19.4 Writing

Level SIX Unit FOUR
Let's learn about school activities!

Choose a name and fill the blanks. You can use several times each name. Then read aloud.

Yesterday

It was a long day at school yesterday.
We were very busy during all the classes.
_____ asked so many questions that _____ explained
all about the Past Tense during our English class again and again.
_____ searched for 20 new verbs in the dictionary during class.
_____ colored the pictures in her notebook, she colors so pretty.
_____ even worked during recess. _____ and I just talked;
we talked about the homework and other things.
The class finally ended at 12 o'clock; so we started
to pick up our things to go home. _____ walked home.
It certainly was a long day at school yesterday.
How was your day at school yesterday? Did you work very hard?

Andy • Harry • Lucy • Miss Patty • Sandy
Tom • Tony

Level SIX Unit FOUR
Let's learn about school activities!

19.5 Language in use

Simple Past Tense of Regular Verbs

We use the simple past tense to describe an action that occurred and was completed in the past. The simple past is formed by adding -ed to the base form of the verb.

Affirmative:
Subject + verb-ed + complement.
Andy asked a lot of questions yesterday.

Interrogative:
Did + subject + verb (NO-ed) + complement.
Did Andy ask a lot of questions yesterday?

Choose the sentence that is correct

1. Which is correct?
   - ☐ Did Andy asked a lot of questions?
   - ☐ Did Andy ask a lot of questions?

2. Which is correct?
   - ☐ Did Miss Patty explain the lesson?
   - ☐ Did Miss Patty explained the lesson?

3. Which is correct?
   - ☐ Did the class ended at 12 o'clock?
   - ☐ Did the class end at 12 o'clock?

4. Which is correct?
   - ☐ Did you and Sandy talk during recess yesterday?
   - ☐ Did you and Sandy talked during recess yesterday?

5. Which is correct?
   - ☐ Did Lucy walked home from school?
   - ☐ Did Lucy walk home from school?

How well did you do in this unit?

Write the CAN DO statement and assess yourself.

Write 3, 2, or 1

3 = VERY WELL

2 = WELL

1 = NOT SO WELL

I CAN...

_____

_____

_____

_____

_____

_____

Level SIX Unit FIVE
Let's learn about action words!

20.1 Vocabulary

Learn the action words

answer — answered

call — called

finish — finished

help — helped

live — lived

open — opened

play — played

stop — stopped

study — studied

visit — visited

want — wanted

watch — watched

20.2 Dialogs

Level SIX Unit FIVE
Let's learn about action words!

Practice the dialogs

Did you call your brother?
- No, I didn't call my brother.
Why not?
- Because I answered the phone.

Did you finish your soup?
-No, I didn't finish it.
Why not?
-Because I wanted a sandwich.

Did you play video games?
- No, I didn't play video games.
Why not?
- Because I studied for the exam.

Did you watch a movie?
-No, I didn't watch a movie.
Why not?
-Because I helped my mom with the dishes.

Did you open the window last night?
-No, I didn't open it last night.
Why not?
-Because my father stopped me.

Did you _____ last night?
No, I didn't _____ .
Why not?
Because _____ .

Now you!

Level SIX Unit FIVE
Let's learn about action words!

20.3 Reading

No mom, I didn't!

My mom is always saying: "Andy this, Andy that!" And of course I have to remember to answer nicely if not, well you know! Yesterday was one of those days… first she said: "Andy did you call your brother for lunch?" No mom, I didn't call him; "why not?" Because I answered the phone first. "OK". Then she said: "Andy, did you finish your soup?" No mom, I didn't finish it; "why not?" Because I wanted a sandwich. "All right". "Andy, did you play video games first?" No mom, I didn't play; I studied for the exam first. "Great!" "Andy, did you watch a movie?" No mom, I didn't watch a movie; I helped with the dishes. "Perfect." "Andy, did you open the window last night?" No mom, I didn't open it; father stopped me. "Right." Later she said: "Andy, did you visit your friend?" No mom, I didn't visit her, she was sick; I just called her. "Good." And finally she said: "I love you Andy." Thanks mom, I love you too!

What did Andy do yesterday? According to the reading answer the questions

1. Did Andy call his brother for lunch?
   ☐ Yes, he called him.
   ☐ No, he didn't call him.

2. Did Andy answer the phone?
   ☐ Yes, he answered the phone
   ☐ No, he didn't answer the phone.

3. Did Andy play video games?
   ☐ Yes, he played.
   ☐ No, he didn't play.

4. Did Andy study for the exam?
   ☐ Yes, he studied for the exam.
   ☐ No, he didn't study for the exam.

5. Did Andy watch a movie?
   ☐ Yes, he watched a movie.
   ☐ No, he didn't watch a movie.

6. Did Andy help with the dishes?
   ☐ Yes, he helped with the dishes.
   ☐ No, he didn't help with the dishes.

7. Did Andy visit his friend?
   ☐ Yes, he visited his friend.
   ☐ No, he didn't visit his friend.

20.4 Writing

Level SIX Unit FIVE
Let's learn about action words!

Choose a verb phrase and fill the blanks. You can use several times each phrase. Then read aloud.

No mom, I didn't!
My mom is always saying: "Andy this, Andy that!"
And of course I have to remember to answer nicely, if not…well you know!
Yesterday was one of those days… first she said:
"Andy did you call your brother for lunch?" No mom, I didn't call him;
"why not?" Because _____. "OK".
Then she said: "Andy, did you finish your soup?" No mom, I didn't finish it;
"why not?" Because _____. "All right".
"Andy, did you play video games first?" No mom,
I didn't play; _____. "Great!"
"Andy, did you watch a movie?" No mom,
I didn't watch a movie; _____. "Perfect."
"Andy, did you open the window last night?" No mom,
I didn't open it _____. "Right."
Later she said: "Andy, did you visit your friend?" No mom,
I didn't visit her, she was sick; _____. "Good."
And finally she said: "I love you Andy." Thanks mom, I love you too!

father stopped me • I answered the phone first •
I helped with the dishes • I just called • I studied for the exam first
I wanted a sandwich

Level SIX Unit FIVE
Let's learn about action words!

We use the simple past tense to describe an action that occurred and was completed in the past.
The simple past is formed by adding -ed to the base form of the verb.

Affirmative:
Subject + verb-ed + complement.
Interrogative:
Did + subject + verb (NO-ed) + complement.
Negative:
Subject + did not = didn't + verb (NO-ed) + complement.

Choose the sentence that is correct

1. Which is correct?
   - Andy didn't open the window.
   - Andy didn't opened the window.
2. Which is correct?
   - Lucy didn't visit her grandparents.
   - Lucy didn't visited her grandparents.
3. Which is correct?
   - Sandy didn't finished her soup.
   - Sandy didn't finish her soup.
4. Which is correct?
   - I didn't play video games.
   - I didn't played video games.
5. Which is correct?
   - Tony didn't called his brother.
   - Tony didn't call his brother.

Tongue Twister Time

I wish to wish the wish you wish to wish,
but if you wish the wish the witch wishes,
I won't wish the wish you wish to wish.

How well did you do in this unit?

Write the CAN DO statement and assess yourself.

Write 3, 2, or 1

3 = VERY WELL
2 = WELL
1 = NOT SO WELL

I CAN...

_____
_____
_____
_____
_____
_____

Level SIX Unit SIX
Let's learn about sports!

21.1 Vocabulary

Learn the sports

21.2 Dialogs

Level SIX Unit SIX
Let's learn about sports!

Practice the dialogs

Did Andy play table tennis last Saturday?
-No, he didn't. He played cricket.

Did Lucy practice martial arts last Friday?
-No, she didn't. She practiced skiing.

Did Tony watch an ice hockey game last Sunday?
-No, he didn't. He watched a rugby game.

Did Sandy train boxing last Thursday?
-No, she didn't. She trained athletics.

Did your friends like the baseball game last Monday?
-No, they didn't. They liked the hockey game.

Did you _____?
No, I didn't. I _____.

Now you!

Level SIX Unit SIX
Let's learn about sports!

21.3 Reading

Incredible sports

My friends and I are very much into sports,
we like the regular sports, but also we like the not so regular sports.
For example: Andy likes cricket and table tennis;
in fact he played cricket last Saturday, he didn't play table tennis.
Lucy loves the martial arts and skiing.
She practiced skiing last Friday but didn't practice martial arts.
Tony likes rugby and ice hockey;
he watched a rugby match from South Africa last Sunday
he says it was fantastic! He didn't watch an ice hockey game.
Sandy is a great athlete she likes boxing also.
She trained athletics on Thursday, but didn't train boxing.
My friends watched sports on TV. They liked the soccer game;
they say the baseball game was boring.
My mom and I like to practice sports together.
We visited the tennis court and we decided to start tennis next week!
What incredible sports do you like?
What sports did you practice last week?

Complete the sentences with the correct sport

1. Andy played _____ but didn't play _____.

2. Lucy practiced _____ but didn't practice _____.

3. Tony watched a _____ match he didn't watch a _____ match.

4. Sandy trained _____ but didn't train _____.

Write (T) for true or (F) for false

1. Andy played table tennis. (____)
2. Lucy practiced martial arts. (____)
3. Tony watched a rugby match. (____)
4. Sandy trained boxing. (____)
5. My friends liked the baseball game. (____)
6. We visited the tennis court. (____)

21.4 Writing

Level SIX Unit SIX
Let's learn about sports!

Choose a sport and fill the blanks. You can use several times each sport. Then read aloud.

Incredible sports

My friends and I are very much into sports, we like the regular sports, but also we like the not so regular sports.
For example: Andy likes _____ and _____.
Lucy loves the _____ and _____.
Tony likes _____ and _____.
Sandy is great. She likes _____ and _____.
My friends watched sports on TV. They liked the _____;
they say the _____ was boring.
My mom and I like to practice sports together.
We visited the tennis court and we decided to start tennis next week!
What incredible sports do you like?
What sports did you practice last week?

cricket • athletics • rugby • ice hockey • table tennis
martial arts • skiing • boxing • baseball • soccer

Level SIX Unit SIX
Let's learn about sports!

21.5 Language in use

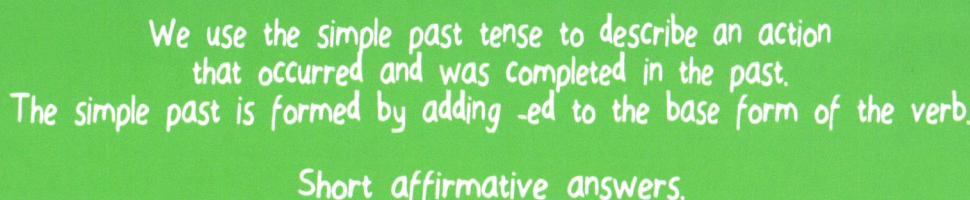

We use the simple past tense to describe an action that occurred and was completed in the past.
The simple past is formed by adding -ed to the base form of the verb.

Short affirmative answers.
Yes, (comma) personal pronoun + did. (period)
Yes, she did.
Short negative answers.
No, (comma) personal pronoun + did not = didn't. (period)
No, he didn't.

Complete the short negative answer

1. Did Andy play table tennis?
   No, _____ _____.

2. Did Lucy practice martial arts?
   No, _____ _____.

3. Did your friends like the baseball game?
   No, _____ _____.

4. Did you and your mom visit the tennis court?
   No, _____ _____.

5. Did you like the rugby match?
   No, _____ _____.

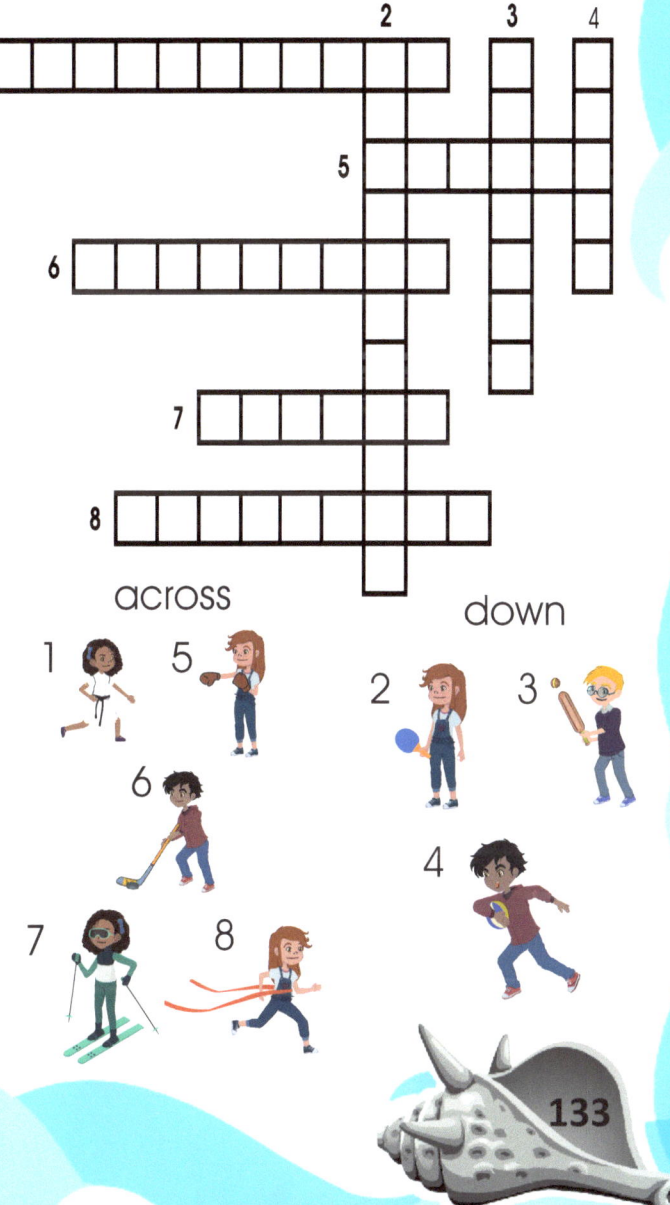

across

down

133

How well did you do in this unit?
Write the CAN DO statement and assess yourself.
Write 3, 2, or 1
3 = VERY WELL
2 = WELL
1 = NOT SO WELL

I CAN...

_____
_____
_____
_____
_____
_____

Level SIX Unit SEVEN
Let's learn about hobbies!

22.1 Vocabulary

Learn the hobbies

baked

delicious

played

relaxing

sewed

beautiful

watched

exciting

painted

incredible

22.2 Dialogs

Level SIX Unit SEVEN
Let's learn about hobbies!

Practice the dialogs

What did Tony do yesterday?
-He baked delicious cookies yesterday.

What did Andy do yesterday?
-He played relaxing music in his guitar.

What did Lucy do yesterday?
-She sewed beautiful clothes for her dolls.

What did Harry do yesterday?
-He watched exciting games.

What did Sandy do yesterday?
-She painted incredible paintings.

What did _____ do yesterday?
She _____.

 Now you!

Level SIX Unit SEVEN
Let's learn about hobbies!

22.3 Reading

Holiday

Yesterday was a special day for our country it was an official holiday so we got a day off from school…Yeah!
What did we do in our day off?
Well, Tony loves to bake. He baked delicious cookies with his mom.
Andy plays all kinds of music, but yesterday he played relaxing music.
His grandparents were there and they enjoyed his music very much.
Lucy has a lot of dolls. She sewed beautiful clothes for all of them.
Harry loves sports. He watched three different exciting games on TV.
I take art class. So I painted incredible paintings yesterday.
Yes, it was a special day yesterday;
no classes and time to enjoy our hobbies.
What did you do in your last holiday? Do you have a special hobby?

What did they do yesterday?

1. What did Sandy do yesterday?
   ☐ sewed ☐ painted ☐ baked
2. What did Andy do yesterday?
   ☐ played guitar
   ☐ watched games
   ☐ painted
3. What did Harry do yesterday?
   ☐ watched games
   ☐ played guitar
   ☐ sewed
4. What did Lucy do yesterday?
   ☐ sewed
   ☐ played guitar
   ☐ painted
5. What did Tony do yesterday?
   ☐ watched games
   ☐ played guitar
   ☐ baked

Write (T) for true or (F) for false

1. Andy played relaxing music.
   (_____)
2. Lucy baked delicious cookies.
   (_____)
3. Harry watched exciting games on TV.
   (_____)
4. Tony sewed clothes.
   (_____)
5. Sandy painted incredible clothes.
   (_____)

22.4 Writing

Level SIX Unit SEVEN
Let's learn about hobbies!

Choose a a name and an adjective. Fill the blanks. You can use several times each word. Just be careful to choose from the correct box. Then read aloud.

Holiday

Yesterday was a special day for our country it was an official holiday so we got a day off from school…Yeah!
What did we do in our day off?
Well, (1) _____ loves to bake. He baked (2) _____ cookies with his mom.
(1) _____ plays all kinds of music,
but yesterday he played (2) _____ music.
His grandparents were there and they enjoyed his music very much.
(1) _____ has a lot of dolls. She sewed (2) _____ clothes for all of them.
(1) _____ loves sports. He watched three different (2) _____ games on TV.
(1) _____ painted (2) _____ paintings yesterday.
Yes, it was a special day yesterday;
no classes and time to enjoy our hobbies.
What did you do in your last holiday? Do you have a special hobby?
I _____ _____ last holiday.

1)
Sandy • Andy • Tony • Harry • Lucy

2)
incredible • exciting • delicious • beautiful • relaxing

Level SIX Unit SEVEN
Let's learn about hobbies!

22.5 Language in use

We use the simple past tense to describe an action that occurred and was completed in the past.
The simple past is formed by adding -ed to the base form of the verb.

Wh- questions

Wh + did + subject + verb (no ED) + complement.

What did Andy play?
He played relaxing music.

Unscramble the sentences

1. _____ _____ _____ _____ ?
   Tony / what / bake / did
2. _____ _____ _____ _____ ?
   Sandy / paint / did / what
3. _____ _____ _____ _____ ?
   sew / Lucy / did / what
4. _____ _____ _____ _____ _____ .
   incredible / games / watched / Harry
5. _____ _____ _____ _____ ?
   music / Andy / relaxing / played

Choose the sentence that is correct

1. Which is correct?
   - What did Tony bake?
   - What did Tony baked?
2. Which is correct?
   - What did Sandy painted?
   - What did Sandy paint?
3. Which is correct?
   - What did Lucy sewed?
   - What did Lucy sew?
4. Which is correct?
   - What did Harry watch?
   - What did Harry watched?
5. Which is correct?
   - What did Andy played?
   - What did Andy play?

How well did you do in this unit?
Write the CAN DO statement and assess yourself.
Write 3, 2, or 1
3 = VERY WELL
2 = WELL
1 = NOT SO WELL

I CAN...

_____
_____
_____
_____
_____
_____

Level SIX Unit EIGHT
Let's learn about languages!

23.1 Vocabulary

Learn the languages and countries

Japan

Japanese

China

Chinese

France

French

Italy

Italian

USA

English

23.2 Dialogs

Level SIX Unit EIGHT
Let's learn about languages!

Practice the dialogs

Guess what!
-What?
I met two people from China.
-From China?
Yes! Their names were Chen and Ping.
They spoke Chinese.
-Cool!

Guess what!
-What?
I met two people from Japan.
-From Japan?
Yes! Their names were Haru and Akari.
They spoke Japanese.
-Cool!

Guess what!
-What?
I met two people from the USA.
-From the USA?
Yes! Their names were Jacob and Emily.
They spoke English.
-Cool!

Guess what!
-What?
I met two people from France.
-From France?
Yes! Their names were Jules and Camille.
They spoke French.
-Cool!

What did _____ do yesterday?
She _____.

Now you!

Level SIX Unit EIGHT
Let's learn about languages!

23.3 Reading

Around the world

My friends and I went to the International Friendship Reunion. There were young people like us from around the world. The purpose was to make new friends and keep in touch with them from that day on. It was awesome! Andy met two young people from China. Their names were Chen and Ping. They spoke Chinese. Lucy met two people from Japan. Their names were Haru and Akari. They spoke Japanese. Sandy met two kids from France. Their names were Jules and Camille. They spoke French. Tony met two friends from Italy. Their names were Pietro and Chiara. They spoke Italian. And I met two young people from the USA. Their names were Jacob and Emily. They spoke English. When the day was over we were very happy with our new friends. We will keep in touch with them forever!

Complete the sentences with the words from the box

1. Andy met people from _____.
   They spoke _____.

2. Lucy met people from _____.
   They spoke _____.

3. Sandy met people from _____.
   They spoke _____.

4. Tony met people from _____.
   They spoke _____.

5. I met people from _____.
   They spoke _____.

Japan / China / France / Italy / USA
Japanese / Chinese / French
Italian / English

Write (T) for true or (F) for false

1. Akari and Haru were from France. (____)

2. Pietro and Chiara spoke English. (____)

3. Jules and Camille were from Italy. (____)

4. Chen and Ping spoke Chinese. (____)

5. Jacob and Emily were from the USA. (____)

23.4 Writing

Level SIX Unit EIGHT
Let's learn about languages!

Choose a country and a language. Fill the blanks. You can use several times each word. Just be careful to choose from the correct box. Then read aloud.

Around the World

My friends and I went to the International Friendship Reunion. There were young people like us from around the world.
The purpose was to make new friends and keep in touch with them from that day on. It was awesome!
Andy met two young people from _____. They spoke _____.
Lucy met two people from _____. They spoke _____.
Sandy met two kids from _____. They spoke _____.
Tony met two friends from _____. They spoke _____.
And I met two young people from the _____. They spoke _____.
When the day was over we were very happy with our new friends.
We will keep in touch with them forever!

1) Japan • China • France • Italy • the USA

2) Japanese • Chinese • French • Italian • English

Level SIX Unit EIGHT
Let's learn about languages!

23.5
Language in use

> We use the simple past tense to describe an action that occurred and was completed in the past.
>
> Simple Past Tense of Irregular Verbs.
> Irregular verbs do not follow normal rules for conjugation.
>
> is - was
> are - were
> meet - met
> speak - spoke

Unscramble the sentences

1. ___ ___ ___ ___ ___ ___ .
   Akari / Japan / and / Haru / from / were

2. ___ ___ ___ ___ ___ .
   Chiara / Italian / Pietro / and / spoke

3. ___ ___ ___ ___ ___ .
   Jules / Camille / Sandy / met / and

4. ___ ___ ___ ___ ___ .
   Chinese / Chen Ping / spoke / and

5. ___ ___ ___ ___ ___ ___ ___ .
   USA / the / were / and / Jacob / Emily / from

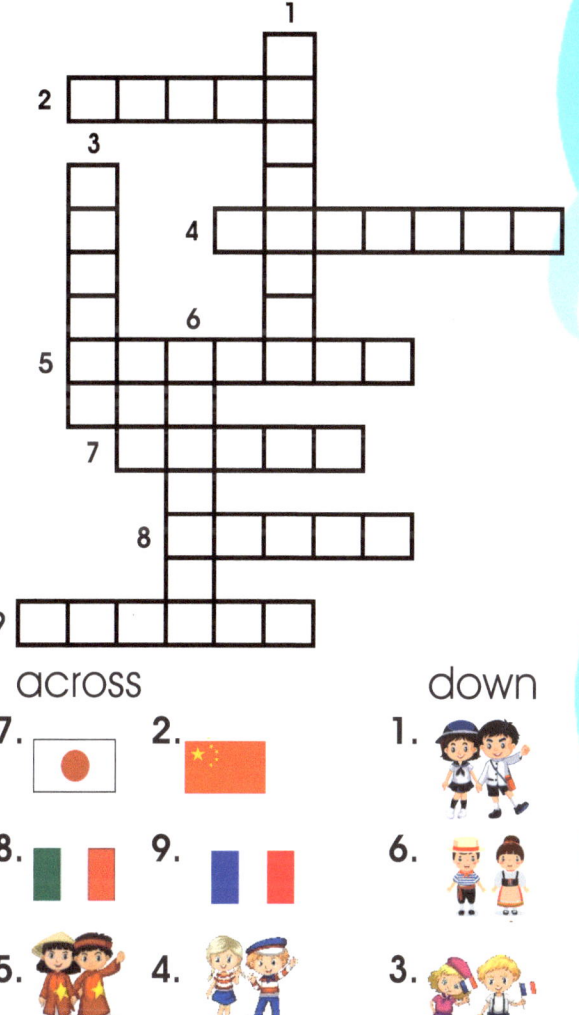

across
7. 🇯🇵
2. 🇨🇳
8. 🇮🇪
9. 🇫🇷
5. 4.

down
1.
6.
3.

145

How well did you do in this unit?
Write the CAN DO statement and assess yourself.
Write 3, 2, or 1
3 = VERY WELL
2 = WELL
1 = NOT SO WELL

I CAN...
_____
_____
_____
_____
_____
_____

Level SIX Unit NINE
Let's learn about the past!

24.1 Vocabulary

Learn the verbs in the past and the jobs

singer — sing / sang

writer — write / wrote

swimmer — swim / swam

teacher — teach / taught

driver — drive / drove

24.2 Dialogs

Level SIX Unit NINE
Let's learn about the past!

Practice the dialogs

What does your father do?
-He is a singer. He sings at a nice restaurant.
Cool!
-He sang at church before.
Nice!

What does your cousin do?
-He is a swimmer. He swims in the beach.
Cool!
-He swam in the pool before.
Nice!

What does your mother do?
-She is a teacher. She teaches math.
Cool!
-She taught science before.
Nice!

What does your grandma do?
-She is a writer. She writes children's stories.
Great!
-She wrote mystery novels before.
Nice!

What does your uncle do?
-He is a driver. He drives buses.
Cool!
-He drove trucks before.
Nice!

What does your _____ do?
-He is a _____. _____.
Cool!
-He _____ _____ before.
Nice!

Level SIX Unit NINE
Let's learn about the past!

24.3 Reading

What do they do?

Miss Patty asked us to talk to our parents and see what jobs our relatives have. So we asked at home, and now we know that they have cool jobs and before that they had awesome jobs too! Sandy's grandma is a writer. She writes children's stories and before that, she wrote mystery novels. Harry's cousin is a swimmer. He swims in the beach and before that, he swam in the pool. Tony's uncle is a driver. He drives buses and before that, he drove trucks. Lucy's mom is a teacher. She teaches math and before that, she taught science. Andy's dad is a singer. He sings at a restaurant and before that, he sang at church. Our parents and relatives for sure have cool jobs! What do your relatives do?

Complete the sentences with the words from the box

1. Who is a writer?
   _____
2. Who is a singer?
   _____
3. Who is a swimmer?
   _____
4. Who is a teacher?
   _____
5. Who is a driver?
   _____

> Harry's cousin
> Sandy's grandma
> Andy's dad / Tony's uncle
> Lucy's mom

Write (T) for true or (F) for false

1. Andy's dad sang at church. (......)
2. Sandy's grandma wrote children's stories. (......)
3. Lucy's mom taught science. (......)
4. Tony's uncle drove buses. (......)
5. Harry's cousin swam in the beach. (......)

24.4 Writing

Level SIX Unit NINE
Let's learn about the past!

Choose a job and an activity. Fill the blanks. You can use several times each word. Just be careful to choose from the correct box. Then read aloud.

What do they do?

Miss Patty asked us to talk to our parents and see what jobs our relatives have. So we asked at home, and now we know that they have cool jobs and before that they had awesome jobs too!
Sandy's grandma is a (1) _____.
She (2) _____ and before that, she (3) _____.
Harry's cousin is a (1) _____. He (2) _____ and before that, he (3) _____. Tony's uncle is a (1) _____.
He (2) _____ and before that, he (3) _____.
Lucy's mom is a (1) _____. She (2) _____ and before that, she (3) _____.
Andy's dad is a (1) _____. He (2) _____ and before that, he (3) _____.
Our parents and relatives for sure have cool jobs!
What do your relatives do?

1) singer • writer • swimmer • teacher • driver

2) sings at a restaurant • drives buses • swims in the beach
teaches math • writes children's stories

3) drove trucks • swam in the pool • wrote mystery novels • taught science • sang at church

Level SIX Unit NINE
Let's learn about the past!

24.5 Language in use

> Simple Past Tense of Irregular Verbs.
> Irregular verbs do not follow normal rules for conjugation.
> We use the same form of the past tense in the affirmative for all subjects.
> Simple Past Tense of Irregular Verbs
> sing - sang
> teach - taught
> swim - swam
> write - wrote
> drive - drove
>
> To change a verb into an agent noun, we simply add "er"
> teach - teacher
> sing - singer

Complete the sentences with the words from the box

driver / singer / teacher
swimmer / writer

1. A person that sings is a _____.
2. A person that teaches is a _____.
3. A person that writes is a _____.
4. A person that swims is a _____.
5. A person that drives is a _____.

Match the verbs

write	drove
teach	met
swim	sang
sing	spoke
meet	swam
speak	taught
drive	wrote

Tongue Twister Time

Swan swim over the sea,
Swim, swan, swim!
Swan swum back again
Well swum, swan!

151

How well did you do in this unit?
Write the CAN DO statement and assess yourself.
Write 3, 2, or 1
3 = VERY WELL
2 = WELL
1 = NOT SO WELL

I CAN...
_____
_____
_____
_____
_____
_____

Level SIX Unit TEN
Let's learn about the city!

25.1
Vocabulary

Learn the activities in the city

have

had

go

went

get

got

buy

bought

take

took

25.2 Dialogs

Level SIX Unit TEN
Let's learn about the city!

Practice the dialogs

Did you go to the library after school?
-Yes, I went to the library.
Did you take out a book?
-Yes, I took out a history book.

Did you go to the supermarket after school?
-Yes, I went to the supermarket.
Did you buy some fruits?
-Yes, I bought some oranges.

Did you go to the mall after school yesterday?
-Yes, I went to the mall.
Did you get a pair of shoes?
-Yes, I got a pair of tennis shoes.

Did you go to the park after school yesterday?
-Yes, I went to the park.
Did you have some ice cream?
-Yes, I had some chocolate ice cream.

Did you go to the movie theater after school yesterday?
-Yes, I went to the movie theater.
Did you watch a funny movie?
-Yes, I watched a funny movie.

Did you go to the _____ after school yesterday?
-Yes, I went to the _____.
Did you _____?
-Yes, I _____.

Now you!

Level SIX Unit TEN
Let's learn about the city!

25.3 Reading

After school

Yesterday was a perfect afternoon. It was nice and warm. So after school my students went with their parents and enjoyed the weather going to different places around the city. Today I want them to tell the class what they did.

Andy will start: "I went to the library and I took out a history book; it was amazing!"

It's Lucy's turn: "I went to the supermarket with my mom we bought some oranges; they were delicious!

It is Tony's turn. "I went to the mall and bought some tennis shoes. They were very comfortable."

Let's listen to Harry. "I went to the park! and of course I had my favorite: chocolate ice cream." And finally, let's listen to Sandy. "I went to the movie theater and I saw a very funny movie."

Well now we know that everybody had a wonderful afternoon around the city.

What did you do after school yesterday?

Complete the sentences with the words from the box

1. Andy went to the _____.
2. Lucy went to the _____.
3. Sandy went to the _____.
4. Tony went to the _____.
5. Harry went to the _____.

library / supermarket
shopping mall / park
movie theater

Write (T) for true or (F) for false

1. Andy took out a geography book from the library. (____)
2. Lucy bought some apples in the supermarket. (____)
3. Sandy saw a scary movie at the movie theater. (____)
4. Tony bought some tennis shoes at the shopping mall. (____)
5. Harry had chocolate ice cream at the park. (____)

Level SIX Unit TEN
Let's learn about the city!

25.4 Writing

Choose an activity and a place. Fill the blanks. You can use several times each word. Be careful to choose from the correct box. Then read aloud.

After school

Yesterday was a perfect afternoon.
It was nice and warm. So after school my students went with their parents and enjoyed the weather.
They will tell us where they went and what they did there.

Andy went to the (1)_____; he (2)_____.
Lucy went to the (1)_____; she (2)_____.
Tony went to the (1)_____; he (2)_____
Harry went to the (1)_____; he (2)_____.
Sandy went to the (1)_____; she (2)_____.
Well everybody certainly enjoyed their afternoon!

What did you do yesterday afternoon?
I went to the _____; and I _____.

---

1) library • supermarket • shopping mall • park • movie theater

2) took out a book • bought fruit • bought shoes
had ice cream • saw a movie

Level SIX Unit TEN
Let's learn about the city!

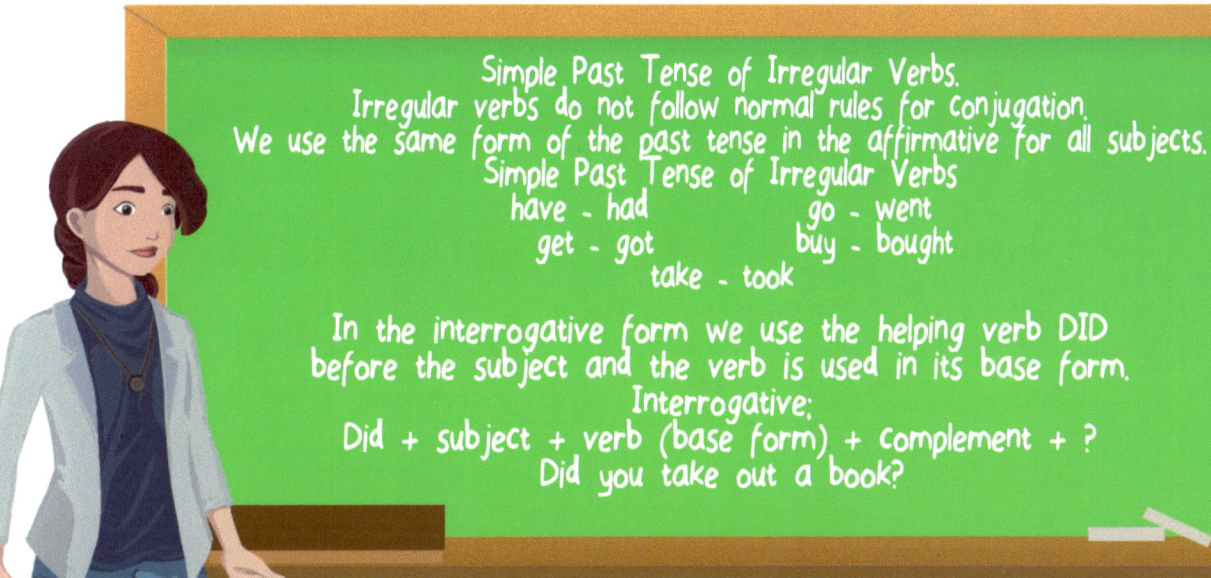

Simple Past Tense of Irregular Verbs.
Irregular verbs do not follow normal rules for conjugation.
We use the same form of the past tense in the affirmative for all subjects.
Simple Past Tense of Irregular Verbs
have - had		go - went
get - got		buy - bought
take - took

In the interrogative form we use the helping verb DID before the subject and the verb is used in its base form.
Interrogative:
Did + subject + verb (base form) + complement + ?
Did you take out a book?

Complete the sentences with the verbs from the box

bought / had / saw / took / went

1. Andy _____ out a history book from the library.
2. Lucy _____ to the supermarket.
3. Sandy _____ a funny movie at the movie theater.
4. Tony _____ some tennis shoes at the shopping mall.
5. Harry _____ chocolate ice cream at the park.

Choose the sentence that is correct

1. Which is correct?
   ☐ Did Andy take out a history book?
   ☐ Did Andy took out a history book?
2. Which is correct?
   ☐ Did Lucy went to the supermarket?
   ☐ Did Lucy go to the supermarket?
3. Which is correct?
   ☐ Did Sandy saw a funny movie?
   ☐ Did Sandy see a funny movie?
4. Which is correct?
   ☐ Did Tony buy tennis shoes?
   ☐ Did Tony bought tennis shoes?
5. Which is correct?
   ☐ Did Harry have chocolate ice cream?
   ☐ Did Harry had chocolate ice cream?

How well did you do in this unit?
Write the CAN DO statement and assess yourself.
Write 3, 2, or 1
3 = VERY WELL
2 = WELL
1 = NOT SO WELL

I CAN...
_____
_____
_____
_____
_____
_____

Level SIX Unit ELEVEN
Let's learn about food!

26.1 Vocabulary

Learn the names of the food

juice   milk

sandwich   hot dog

chicken

fish   hamburger   water

26.2 Dialogs

Level SIX Unit ELEVEN
Let's learn about food!

Practice the dialogs

Did you drink milk at school?
-No, I didn't drink milk. I drank orange juice.
OK!

Did you drink apple juice at school?
-No, I didn't drink apple juice. I drank water.
OK!

Did you eat fish at school?
-No, I didn't eat fish. I ate chicken.
OK!

Did you buy a sandwich at school?
-No, I didn't buy a sandwich.
I bought a hot dog.
OK!

Did you have a hamburger at school?
- No, I didn't have a hamburger.
 I had a sandwich.
OK!

Did you _____ _____ at school?
-No, I didn't _____ _____.
I _____
OK!

Now you!

Level SIX Unit ELEVEN
Let's learn about food!

Food

We always have delicious food to pick from at the school cafeteria to have for lunch. The problem is deciding what we want, everything is always so delicious! Today for example, Sandy didn't drink milk; she drank fresh orange juice.
Andy didn't eat fish. He said that he ate fish yesterday so he ate chicken instead.
Lucy loves hot dogs so she bought a hot dog; she didn't buy a sandwich.
Harry likes the sandwiches from school, so he had a sandwich. He didn't have a hamburger today.
And I was so thirsty that I drank only water, I didn't drink the apple juice I had in my lunch box. Yes, everything in my school cafeteria is so delicious it is sometimes difficult to decide what to get.
What did you get for lunch at your school cafeteria today?

Choose the correct answer

1. Did Sandy drink milk at school?
   ☐ Yes, she drank milk.
   ☐ No, she didn't drink milk.
2. Did Andy eat chicken at school?
   ☐ Yes, he ate chicken
   ☐ No, he didn't eat chicken.
3. Did Lucy buy a sandwich at school?
   ☐ Yes, she bought a sandwich.
   ☐ No, she didn't buy a sandwich.
4. Did Harry have a sandwich at school?
   ☐ Yes, he had a sandwich.
   ☐ No, he didn't have a sandwich.
5. Did Tony drink apple juice at school?
   ☐ Yes, he drank apple juice.
   ☐ No, he didn't drink apple juice.

Choose the food and complete the sentences

1. Harry had _____ at school.
   • a sandwich   • a hamburger
   • chicken
2. Tony drank _____ at school.
   • milk   • water   • orange juice
3. Andy ate _____ at school.
   • fish   • a sandwich
   • chicken
4. Sandy drank _____ at school.
   • milk   • orange juice
   • apple juice
5. Lucy bought _____ at school.
   • sandwich   • water
   • hot dog

26.4 Writing

Choose a food. Fill the blanks. You can use several times each word. Then read aloud.

> **Food**
> We always have delicious food to pick from at the school cafeteria to have for lunch.
> The problem is deciding what we want, everything is always so delicious!
> Today for example, Sandy didn't have _____; she had _____.
> Andy didn't eat _____, so he ate _____ instead.
> Lucy bought _____; she didn't buy _____.
> Harry had _____. He didn't have a _____ today.
> Tony had _____, I didn't have _____.
> Yes, everything in my school cafeteria is so delicious it is sometimes difficult to decide what to get.
> What did you get for lunch at your school cafeteria today?
> I _____.

a sandwich • a hamburger • a hot dog • fish • chicken
water • orange juice • apple juice • milk • yogurt

Level SIX Unit ELEVEN
Let's learn about food!

26.5 Language in use

Simple Past Tense of irregular verbs.
Negative form:
I didn't drink, You didn't drink,
He, she, it, didn't drink, We didn't drink
They didn't drink

In the negative form we use
the helping verb DID + NOT (didn't) and the base form of the verb.
Negative:
Subject + didn't + verb (base form) + complement.
Harry didn't have a hamburger.

Complete the sentences with the negative past tense form of the verbs in parenthesis.

Example:

Harry _____ a hot dog. (not buy)

Harry didn't buy a hot dog.

1. Sandy _____ milk. (not drink)
2. Tony _____ water. (not buy)
3. Andy _____ fish. (not eat)
4. Lucy _____ chicken. (not have)
5. Harry _____ a sandwich. (not get)

Choose the sentence that is correct

1. Which is correct?
   ☐ Sandy didn't drink milk.
   ☐ Sandy didn't drank milk.
2. Which is correct?
   ☐ Andy didn't eat fish.
   ☐ Andy didn't ate fish.
3. Which is correct?
   ☐ Lucy didn't buy a hot dog.
   ☐ Lucy didn't bought a hot dog.
4. Which is correct?
   ☐ Harry didn't had a hamburger.
   ☐ Harry didn't have a hamburger.
5. Which is correct?
   ☐ Tony didn't got a sandwich.
   ☐ Tony didn't get a sandwich.

How well did you do in this unit?
Write the CAN DO statement and assess yourself.
Write 3, 2, or 1
3 = VERY WELL
2 = WELL
1 = NOT SO WELL

I CAN...

_____
_____
_____
_____
_____
_____

Level SIX Unit TWELVE
Let's learn about animals!

27.1
Vocabulary

Learn the names of the animals

27.2 Dialogs

Practice the dialogs

I went to the zoo last Sunday.
-Really? Did you see a bear?
Yes, I did. It was huge.

I went to the zoo last Sunday.
-Really? Did you see a tiger?
No, I didn't. But I saw a lion.

I went to the zoo last Sunday.
-Really? Did you see a parrot?
Yes, I did. It was colorful.

I went to the zoo last Sunday.
-Really? Did you see a hawk?
No, I didn't. But I saw an eagle.

I went to the zoo last Sunday.
-Really? Did you see a shark?
Yes, I did. It was scary.

I went to the zoo last Sunday.
-Really? Did you see an octopus?
No, I didn't. But I saw a dolphin.

I went to the zoo last Sunday.
-Really? Did you see a/an _____?
No, I didn't. Yes, I did.

Now you!

Level SIX Unit TWELVE
Let's learn about animals!

27.3 Reading

At the zoo

Last Sunday my family and I went to the zoo, it was fantastic! I saw many incredible animals. Some live in the water, like the octopus. Some live in the air, like the eagle. And some live on the land, like the horse.
I loved the animals that live in the water; my favorite is the dolphin. My friends at school were asking me about the animals that I saw. So I told them that first I saw a huge bear. Then a colorful parrot. Next a scary shark. Then I saw a lion, an eagle and finally the animal I really wanted to see: a dolphin!
The animals I didn't see were: a tiger, a hawk and an octopus. Maybe next time that I go to the zoo I will see these animals too. What are your favorite animals from the land, water or air?

Choose the correct answer

1. Did Harry see a bear?
   ☐ Yes, he did.
   ☐ No, he didn't.
2. Did Harry see a tiger?
   ☐ Yes, he did.
   ☐ No, he didn't.
3. Did Harry see a parrot?
   ☐ Yes, he did.
   ☐ No, he didn't.
4. Did Harry see a hawk?
   ☐ Yes, he did.
   ☐ No, he didn't.
5. Did Harry see a dolphin?
   ☐ Yes, he did.
   ☐ No, he didn't.

Write the answer

1. What animal did Harry want to see?
   _____.
2. What animal did he see first?
   _____.
3. What animal that lives in the air Harry didn't see?
   _____.
4. What animal was colorful?
   _____.
5. What animal was scary?
   _____.

27.4 Writing

Level SIX Unit TWELVE
Let's learn about animals!

Choose any animal. Fill the blanks. You can use several times each word. Then read aloud.

At the zoo

Last Sunday my family and I went to the zoo,
it was fantastic! I saw many incredible animals.
Some live in the water, like the _____.
Some live in the air, like the _____.
And some live on the land, like the _____.
I loved the animals that live in the _____; my favorite is the _____.
My friends at school were asking me about the animals that I saw.
So I told them that first I saw a _____. Then a _____.
Next a _____. Then I saw a _____, a/an _____ and finally
the animal I really wanted to see: a/an _____!
The animals I didn't see were: a/an _____, a/an _____ and a/an _____.
Maybe next time that I go to the zoo I will see these animals too.
What are your favorite animals from the land, water or air?

shark • dolphin • octopus • parrot • eagle
hawk • tiger • lion • bear • horse

Level SIX Unit TWELVE
Let's learn about animals!

27.5 Language in use

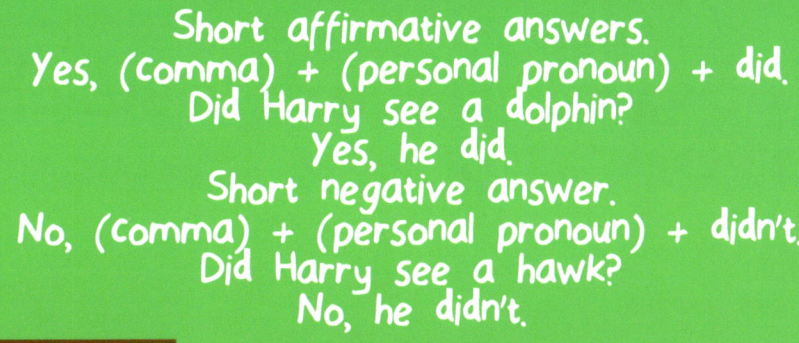

Simple Past Tense of irregular verbs.

Short affirmative answers.
Yes, (comma) + (personal pronoun) + did.
Did Harry see a dolphin?
Yes, he did.
Short negative answer.
No, (comma) + (personal pronoun) + didn't.
Did Harry see a hawk?
No, he didn't.

Write the correct short negative answer

1. Did you see a shark?
____, _____ _____.
2. Did Sandy see a parrot?
____, _____ _____.
3. Did Harry see a horse?
____, _____ _____.
4. Did you and Harry see an octopus?
____, _____ _____.
5. Did Lucy and Tony see a bear?
____, _____ _____.

Choose the short answer that is correct

Which answer is correct?
1. Did Harry see a horse?
   • Yes he did
   • No, he didn't.
2. Did you see a hawk?
   • Yes, I did.
   • No I didn't
3. Did you and Harry see an octopus?
   • Yes we did
   • No, we didn't.
4. Did Lucy and Tony see a bear?
   • Yes, they did.
   • No they didn't
5. Did Sandy see a parrot?
   • Yes, she did.
   • No she didn't

How well did you do in this unit?
Write the CAN DO statement and assess yourself.
Write 3, 2, or 1
3 = VERY WELL
2 = WELL
1 = NOT SO WELL

I CAN...
_____
_____
_____
_____
_____
_____

Level SIX Unit THIRTEEN
Let's learn about actions!

28.1 Vocabulary

Learn the action words

write / wrote

sing / sang

cut / cut

feed / fed

drink / drank

read / read

drive / drove

171

28.2 Dialogs

Practice the dialogs

What did you do at school this week?
-I wrote a poem.
Where did you write it?
-I wrote it in my notebook.
When did you write it?
-I wrote it on Tuesday.
Good job!

What did you do at school this week?
-I sang a song.
Where did you sing?
-I sang in the school assembly.
When did you sing?
-I sang on Monday.
Good job!

What did you do at school this week?
-I read a book.
Where did you read it?
-I read it in the library.
When did you read it?
-I read it on Thursday.
Good job!

What did you do at school this week?
-I _____.
Where did you _____?
-I _____.
When did you _____?
-I _____.
Good job!

Now you!

Level SIX Unit THIRTEEN
Let's learn about actions!

28.3 Reading

What did you do at school?

It was a very active week at school. All the students in my class had something important to do.

On Monday they sang songs; Tony sang in the school assembly. He was great.

On Tuesday it was writing in your notebook day; Andy wrote a beautiful poem. Also on Tuesday during recess was very exciting, the children drove their box cars all around the yard; Harry won the race.

On Wednesday we fixed the classroom up with the decorations the children cut out; Lucy's decorations were beautiful.

On Thursday we all went to the library; we all read books there. And on Friday it was Sandy's turn to feed the class hamster; she really likes that hamster.

It was certainly a very active week for all the students in my class. What did you do at school this week?

Choose the correct answer

1. What did Andy do on Tuesday?
   - wrote a poem
   - sang a song
   - read a book
2. What did Tony do on Monday?
   - wrote a poem
   - sang a song
   - read a book
3. What did Lucy do on Thursday?
   - wrote a poem
   - sang a song
   - read a book
4. What did Sandy do on Friday?
   - cut out decorations
   - fed the hamster
   - drove a box car
5. What did Harry do on Tuesday?
   - cut out decorations
   - fed the hamster
   - drove a box car

Write the complete answer

1. Who sang in the school assembly?
   _____.

2. When did Andy write a beautiful poem?
   _____.

3. Where did they drive the box cars?
   _____.

4. What did the children do on Wednesday?
   _____.

28.4 Writing

Level SIX Unit THIRTEEN
Let's learn about actions!

Choose any school activity. Fill the blanks. You can use several times each word. Then read aloud.

What did you do at school?

It was a very active week at school.
All the students in my class had something important to do.
On Monday Tony _____ .
On Tuesday Andy _____ .
Also on Tuesday during recess was very exciting, Harry _____ .
On Wednesday Lucy _____ .
On Thursday everybody _____ .
And on Friday Sandy _____ .
It was certainly a very active week for all the students in my class.
What did you do at school this week?
I _____ .

---

wrote a poem • sang a song • read a book
fed the hamster • cut out decorations • drove a box car

Level SIX Unit THIRTEEN
Let's learn about actions!

28.5 Language in use

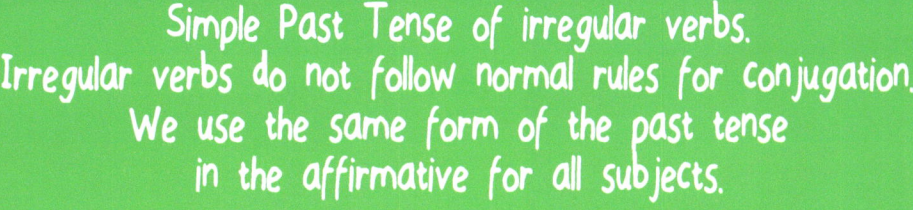

Simple Past Tense of irregular verbs.
Irregular verbs do not follow normal rules for conjugation.
We use the same form of the past tense
in the affirmative for all subjects.

WH - questions:
What + did + subject + verb (base form) + complement?
What did you do last week?

Tongue Twister Time

How many cookies could
A good cook cook,
If a good cook
Could cook cookies?
A good cook
Could cook
As much cookies
As a good cook who
could cook cookies.

Unscramble the sentences

1. ___ ___ ___ ___ ___ ___?
   did / do / at / what / you / school
2. ___ ___ ___ ___ ___?
   it / sing / where / did / you
3. ___ ___ ___ ___ ___?
   it / write / you / did / when
4. ___ ___ ___ ___ ___?
   drive / it / you / where / did
5. ___ ___ ___ ___ ___?
   When / it / feed / did / you

How well did you do in this unit?
Write the CAN DO statement and assess yourself.
Write 3, 2, or 1
3 = VERY WELL
2 = WELL
1 = NOT SO WELL

I CAN...
_____
_____
_____
_____
_____
_____

Level SIX Unit FOURTEEN
Let's learn about hobbies!

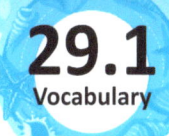

Learn the hobbies

roller skate

skateboard

read

swim

cook

paint

play

29.2 Dialogs

Level SIX Unit FOURTEEN
Let's learn about hobbies!

Practice the dialogs

Could you roller skate when you were six years old?
-No, I couldn't.
-But now I can roller skate perfectly.

Could you skateboard when you were six years old?
-No, I couldn't.
-But now I can skateboard perfectly.

Could you swim when you were six years old?
-No, I couldn't.
-But now I can swim perfectly.

Could you cook when you were six years old?
-No, I couldn't.
-But now I can cook perfectly.

Could you read when you were five years old?
-No, I couldn't.
But now I can read perfectly.

Could you _____ when you were _____ years old?
-No, I couldn't.
-But now I can _____ perfectly.

Now you!

Level SIX Unit FOURTEEN
Let's learn about hobbies!

29.3 Reading

Remember…

All the students in my class have hobbies and they are good at their hobbies now; but what about when they were 5 or 6 years old? I asked them if they remember. Sandy remembers that she couldn't roller skate when she was six years old but now she can roller skate perfectly. Lucy remembers she couldn't skateboard and now she can skateboard so fast.

Tony remembers that when he was six he couldn't swim; he was afraid of the water but now he loves to swim! Harry remembers that it was difficult for him to read at five years old, and now he can read entire books. Andy remembers that when he was six years old he wanted to play the guitar and just couldn't. But now he knows many songs.

Oh yes, my students remember what they couldn't do when they were six years old but now they can do so many things; I am so proud of them! I know they will learn a lot of new things in the future.

Complete the sentences with the expressions from the box

1. Tony _____ when he was six years old.

2. Harry _____ when he was five years old.

3. Sandy _____ when she was six years old.

4. Lucy _____ when she was six years old.

5. Andy _____ the guitar when he was six years old.

Couldn't…
play the guitar / read / roller skate
skateboard / swim

Answer the questions according to the reading

1. Could Andy swim when he was six years old?
   _____.

2. Could Lucy roller skate when she was six years old?
   _____.

3. Could Harry read when he was five years old?
   _____.

4. Could Tony swim when he was six years old?
   _____.

5. Could Sandy cook when she was six years old?
   _____.

29.4 Writing

Level SIX Unit FOURTEEN
Let's learn about hobbies!

Choose any hobby. Fill the blanks. You can use several times each word. Then read aloud.

What did you do at school?

It was a very active week at school. All the students in my class had something important to do.
On Monday Tony _____.
On Tuesday Andy _____.
Also on Tuesday during recess was very exciting, Harry _____.
On Wednesday Lucy _____.
On Thursday everybody _____.
And on Friday Sandy _____.
It was certainly a very active week for all the students in my class.
What did you do at school this week?
I _____.

wrote a poem / sang a song / read a book
fed the hamster / cut out decorations / drove a box car

Level SIX Unit FOURTEEN
Let's learn about hobbies!

29.5 Language in use

> We use COULD to express general ability in the past.
> We use COULDN'T (could+not) to express the lack of ability in the past.
>
> Affirmative:
> Sandy could roller skate when she was eight years old.
> Negative:
> Harry couldn't read when he was five years old.
> Interrogative:
> Could you swim when you were six years old?

Choose the correct short answer from the box below

1. Could Sandy roller skate?
   ___, _____ _____.
2. Could you skateboard?
   _____
3. Could Harry and Andy play the guitar?
   ___, _____ _____.
4. Could you and Lucy swim in the pool?
   ___, _____ _____.
5. Could Tony read a complete book?
   ___, _____ _____.

Unscramble the sentences

1. ___ ___ ___ ___ ___?.
   guitar / the / could / play / you
2. ___ ___ ___ ___ ___?.
   roller / skate / you / could / fast
3. ___ ___ ___ ___ ___ ___ .
   Tony / swim / the / pool / in / couldn't
4. ___ ___ ___ ___ ___ .
   couldn't / the / park / skateboard / Lucy / in
5. ___ ___ ___ ___ ___ .
   food / delicious / could / Sandy / cook

How well did you do in this unit?
Write the CAN DO statement and assess yourself.
Write 3, 2, or 1
3 = VERY WELL
2 = WELL
1 = NOT SO WELL

I CAN...
_____
_____
_____
_____
_____
_____

Level SIX Unit FIFTEEN
Let's learn about polite expressions!

Learn the polite expressions

listen

open

point

sit down

stand up

open

close

repeat

30.2 Dialogs

Level SIX Unit FIFTEEN
Let's learn about polite expressions!

Practice the dialogs

Let's start the class! Would you please listen?
-Yes, of course.
Thank you!

Let's continue! Would you please repeat after me?
-Sure.
Thanks!

Sandy, would you please point to the answer?
-Certainly.
Good job!

Would you all please stand up?
-Sure.
Perfect!

Andy, would you please close the door?
-Certainly.
Thank you!

Would you please, open your book?
-Yes, of course.
Great!

Now you!

Would you please, _____?
-Yes, of course.
Great!

Level SIX Unit FIFTEEN
Let's learn about polite expressions!

Would you… please?

Today was the day of being polite; so I asked my students to ask and respond very politely to anything they needed, ALL day long!

It was a nice day. We were all being nice to each other. We learned that if we ask for things politely we would get what we needed easier; we would not fight and we would not get angry at each other. And it worked! I said to my students: "Would please close the door?" and they answered: "Certainly!" It was nice to hear everybody being nice to each other. We learned to use the expression: "Would you please…? To ask for something or a favor. What else did we learn? We learned to answer; Certainly! Sure! Of course! And the most magic words ever: Thank you!

Do you and your friends use these expressions in class?

What is your favorite polite expression? Would you please tell me?

Match the polite expressions with the pictures

a) Would you please listen?
   -Yes, of course.
   Thank you!
b) Would you please repeat after me?
   -Sure.
   Thanks!
c) Sandy, would you please point to the answer?
   -Certainly.
   Good job!
d) Would you please, open your book?
   -Yes, of course.
   Great!
e) Would you all please stand up?
   -Sure.
   Perfect!

30.4 Writing

Level SIX Unit FIFTEEN
Let's learn about polite expressions!

Would you… please?

Here are some useful polite expressions to learn and use in the classroom:

1. _____ you please _____?
   -Yes, _____.
   _____!
   Thank you/ listen/of course/ would

2. _____ you please, ____ your book?
   -Yes, _____.
   _____!
   Great/ of course/ open/ would

3. ____ you please ____ the door?
   - _____ .
   _____!
   Thank you/ close/would/certainly

186

Level SIX Unit FIFTEEN
Let's learn about polite expressions!

We use Would as modal auxiliary verb to express desire, polite requests, questions, opinion, hope, wish and regret.
WOULD has invariable only one form. The main verb is usually in the base form.

Affirmative:
Subject + would + verb (base form)
I would like some water, please.

Interrogative:
Would + subject + verb
Would you sit down please?

Tongue Twister Time

How much wood would
A woodchuck chuck
If a woodchuck
Could chuck wood?
He would chuck,
He would,
As much as he could,
And chuck
As much wood
As a woodchuck would
If a woodchuck
Could chuck wood.

R	D	L	U	O	W	C	M	Y	C
E	O	P	E	N	O	E	L	O	L
Q	N	I	M	U	S	N	U	C	O
U	V	Z	R	A	I	L	F	D	S
E	R	S	E	A	D	H	D	F	E
S	E	L	T	N	E	T	S	I	L
T	P	R	E	S	P	O	N	S	E
U	E	P	X	P	O	L	I	T	E
C	A	W	I	N	D	O	W	B	Z
B	T	J	S	K	N	A	H	T	H

CERTAINLY   POLITE
CLOSE   REPEAT
COULD   REQUEST
COURSE   RESPONSE
LISTEN   THANKS
OPEN   WINDOW
PLEASE   WOULD

How well did you do in this unit?
Write the CAN DO statement and assess yourself.
Write 3, 2, or 1
3 = VERY WELL
2 = WELL
1 = NOT SO WELL

I CAN...
_____
_____
_____
_____
_____
_____

REFERENCES

- Communicative Language Learning. Retrieved August 23, 2019 from:
  http://www.educationbridge-id.com/news-a-article/72-communicative-language-teaching-clt.html

- Brown, H. Douglas (1994). Principles of Language Learning and Teaching. Prentice Hall.

- Beale, Jason (2008). Is communicative language teaching a thing of the past?. TESOL article.

- Harmer, Jeremy (2007). How to teach English. Pearson Longman.

- Richards, Jack C (2002). Methodology in Language Teaching. Cambridge University Press.

- Willis, Jane (1996). A Framework for Task-Based Learning. Longman.

- Hermitt, A. (2015). Spiral Learning, a superior approach? *In Families.com*. Retrieved January 9th, 2015, from http://www.families.com/blog/spiral-learning-a-superior approach.

- Fleming, N. Baume, D. (2006) Learning Styles.

- Again: VARKing up the right tree!, Educational Developments, SEDA Ltd, Issue 7.4 Nov. 2006.

- Harmer, Jeremy. How to *Teach English*. Harlow: Longman, 1998. Krashen, Stephen D., and Terrell, Tracy D. The *Natural Approach*. Oxford: Pergamon, 1983.

- Sökmen, Anita J. "Current Trends in Teaching Second Language Vocabulary". *In Vocabulary: Description, Acquisition and Pedagogy,* edited by N. Schmitt and M. McCarthy, 237-257 England: Cambridge University Press, 1997.

- Snow, Marguerite Ann. *"Teaching English as a Second or Foreign Language".* In Content-Based and Immersion Models for Second and Foreign Language Teaching" Edited by M. Celce-Murcia. Heinle & Heinle Thomson Learning, 2001.

- Roth, Genevieve. *Teaching Very Young Children*. Richmond Handbooks for English Teachers. London: Richmond Publishing. 1998.

- freepik.com (website). This website is operated by Freepik Company, S.L., registered in the Commercial Registry of Málaga, volume 4994, sheet 217, page number MA-113059, with Tax Number B-93183366 and registered office at 13 Molina Lario St., 5th floor, 29015, Málaga, Spain ("Company"). All intellectual property rights over the Website, the Services, and/or the Freepik Content, its design, and source code, and all content included in any of them (including without limitation text, images, animations, databases, graphics, logos, trademarks, icons, buttons, pictures, videos, sound recordings, etc.) belong or are licensed to the Company.

ABOUT THE AUTHOR

Patricia Avila has been an English teacher for more than 45 years in her native Tijuana, B. C. She has a Bachelor's in Education from the National Pedagogical University (UPN).

Her experience as a teacher ranges from Kindergarten to Masters. She has functioned as coordinator of Bachelor's in ESL Teaching, as well as for various other universities; she has also worked as an Academic Consultant for different Publishing Houses for more than 15 years. Her wide experience and love for young learners has given her the opportunity to share with you SMART DOLPHIN ZONE, a series that will enhance the learning of English in a **dynamic** and **fun** way.

METHODOLOGIES:
- Vocabulary learning
- Communicative Language Learning
- Integrated Skills Approach
- Spiral Learning
- Topic Based Approach

FEATURES:
- Each book with 30 units
- Two different levels in each book
- Each unit has five lessons:
    - Lesson 1: Vocabulary
    - Lesson 2: Dialogs
    - Lesson 3: Reading
    - Lesson 4: Writing
    - Lesson 5: Language in Use
- **Special features:**
    Songs, rhymes, jokes for kids, advertisements, classical stories, fables, movie reviews, short biographies, short classical stories, story fragments and weather forecasts.

Interested in purchasing a platform that is the perfect match for this book?
Email us: books@unilxeducation.com

www.ingramcontent.com/pod-product-compliance
Lightning Source LLC
Chambersburg PA
CBHW041949240426
43668CB00034B/16